Miriam B. Loo's

All-Occasion Appetizers

Recipes Compiled by Miriam B. Loo

Photographer—Ron Oatney
Food Stylist—Marjorie Read

D1445615

Born and raised in Topeka, Kansas, MIRIAM BAKER LOO is an accomplished businesswoman and creative homemaker who has been an enthusiastic cook since her youth. After her graduation from Washburn University of Topeka, from which she recently received the Outstanding Achievement Award, she married Orin Loo, an artist and lithographer. The Loo family later moved to Colorado Springs, Colorado, where in 1950, with the help of her husband, Miriam founded Current, Inc.

Current® is a national mail order firm which has grown from a basement business in the Loo home, when the product line included Post-A-Note® cards and recipe cards designed by Mr. Loo, to a thriving enterprise serving millions of customers.

Miriam Loo introduced recipes into the Current line by including them on note cards and calendars, and now the company publishes several cookbooks each year. In 1979, she established the Current Test Kitchen, which today includes four kitchens and a staff of six home economists who carefully test each Current recipe. She attends gourmet cooking classes and makes public appearances on behalf of Current all over the country, yet she still enjoys cooking and entertaining for her family (including three grown sons and five grandchildren) and friends.

Long involved in volunteer activities, Miriam Loo has received national recognition for her accomplishments in community work, church leadership and business.

Dear Friend,

In planning menus for large and small groups for all kinds of occasions, I've learned that a collection of good "appetizer" recipes is a hostess' best friend. For this reason, I've grouped all sorts of recipes together in this book to provide you with the greatest versatility for your entertaining needs. There are fancy first courses for formal sit-down dinners, light tea sandwiches for afternoon gatherings and out-of-hand nibbles for un-planned or informal get-togethers. You'll be able to find something to suit every social engagement on your calendar!

A buffet of light and hearty hors d'oeuvres and appetizers is one of my favorite ways of entertaining these days, and I try to make my table as attractive as possible. These kinds of foods can be the showiest and the most fun to prepare. The right combination of foods and dishes is im-portant, but creative garnishes really complete the job. You'll find several easy ones illustrated and photographed here that you might want to try.

Whether you're planning an elaborate feast or a simple visit with a few friends, keep this book handy. I hope it will make your task easier, tastier and more fun.

Sincerely,

Miriam B. Loo

TABLE OF CONTENTS

chapter 1 CONTENTS

First Courses   *Page*

Pictured on the preceding page is Artichokes a la Béarnaise.

ARTICHOKES A LA BÉARNAISE

"This saucy appetizer can be tricky to eat, but well worth the effort. Serve it before a roast, steak or broiled fish."

2 artichokes . . . . Trim stems from artichokes. Cut 1 inch off the top.
Fresh lemon juice Pull off the bottom row of leaves and, with kitchen
Boiling water shears, cut off the sharp leaf tips. Rinse thoroughly.
1 tsp. salt Rub cut edges with lemon juice to prevent darken-
ing. Place artichokes in a 3-quart saucepan; cover
with boiling water. Add salt, cover and bring to a boil;
reduce heat to low and simmer for 30 to 40 minutes
or until a leaf pulls out easily. Remove artichokes
with a slotted spoon and drain upside-down.

1 egg . . . . In a small saucepan, lightly beat the egg. Add may-
½ c. real mayonnaise onnaise, lemon juice, parsley, onion, mustard and
1 tbsp. fresh lemon tarragon; stir until well blended. Cook and stir over
juice low heat for 5 minutes or until thickened (do not boil).
2 tsp. minced fresh Remove from heat.
parsley
½ tsp. grated onion
¼ tsp. Dijon mustard
¼ tsp. dried tarragon
leaves, crushed

1 tbsp. real butter . . . . . Stir in butter until butter melts and mixture is well
blended. Keep warm over hot, not boiling, water.

Lettuce leaves . . . . . . To serve, cut each artichoke in half lengthwise.
Lemon wedges Remove choke. Place halves on lettuce leaves.
Spoon 1 to 2 tablespoons of the sauce onto each half.
Garnish with lemon. Pass the remaining sauce
or serve in individual small bowls. Have extra napkins
and use finger bowls (see page 13), if desired.

Makes 4 servings

7

TRIMMING ARTICHOKES

Select artichokes with tightly closed but not curled leaves. Cut the stem straight across so the artichoke can stand. Turn on its side and cut 1 inch off the top with a sharp knife. Pull off the bottom row of leaves and, with kitchen shears, cut off the spiny tips of the remaining leaves. Rinse thoroughly. Rub the cut edges with lemon juice. The choke can be removed before or after cooking. Spread the top leaves apart and pull out the center cluster of leaves. Scrape out the hairy choke with a grapefruit spoon.

MARINATED ANTIPASTO VEGETABLES

1 c. small .... cauliflowerets
1 med. carrot, cut in ½" sticks
¼ lb. fresh mushrooms, sliced
1 med. zucchini, cut in 1½" sticks
½ pkg. (9 oz.) frozen Italian cut green beans, thawed

In a medium saucepan, cover cauliflower with water. Over medium-high heat, bring to a boil; reduce heat to low and simmer for 7 minutes or until crisp-tender. Drain well and place in a 2-quart bowl or casserole to cool. Repeat process with carrot and cook for 5 minutes or until crisp-tender; drain and add to cauliflower to cool. Add mushrooms, zucchini and green beans.

⅔ c. vegetable oil .....
⅓ c. fresh lemon juice
2 tbsp. water
2 tbsp. chopped onion
2 tsp. sugar
1 clove garlic, minced
1 tsp. dried basil leaves, crushed
¾ tsp. salt
¼ tsp. freshly ground pepper

Place oil, lemon juice, water, onion, sugar, garlic, basil, salt and pepper in a blender container; cover and blend until uniform. Pour marinade over vegetables and toss to coat. Cover and refrigerate at least 4 hours or overnight, stirring occasionally.

1 jar (2 oz.) whole ....
pimientos, drained and coarsely chopped

To serve, add pimientos and toss to mix well. Drain and serve small portions on individual antipasto plates (see page 9).

Makes about 5¼ cups

NOTES:

CAPONATA

"Add this unusual, relish-like mixture to your Italian dinner as part of the antipasto or with the entrée. Serve it with a pasta dish that has a creamy sauce rather than tomato sauce."

1 med. eggplant, ... **peeled and diced in ½" pieces** **1 tsp. salt**	Place eggplant in a large bowl and toss with salt; let stand for 10 minutes. Drain.
½ c. sliced celery ...... **4 tbsp. vegetable oil or olive oil** **½ c. chopped onion**	In a 10-inch skillet over medium heat, sauté celery in 2 tablespoons oil for 5 minutes. Add onion and sauté for 5 minutes or until soft. Remove with a slotted spoon to a small bowl; set aside. Add remaining 2 tablespoons oil to skillet and sauté eggplant for 10 minutes or until lightly browned, stirring gently.
1 can (16 oz.) .... **whole tomatoes, drained and coarsely chopped** **¼ c. sliced ripe olives** **2 tbsp. capers, drained** **1 tbsp. red wine vinegar** **½ tsp. sugar** **¼ tsp. salt** **⅛ tsp. freshly ground pepper**	Add celery mixture, tomatoes, olives, capers, vinegar, sugar, salt and pepper. Bring to a boil; reduce heat to low and simmer, uncovered, for 15 minutes or until eggplant is tender. Taste for additional seasoning. Cool, cover and chill.

To serve, use small portions as part of individual antipasto plates (see below).

Makes 4 cups

ARRANGING ANTIPASTO

Antipasto is usually composed of cold meat, fish, cheese and vegetables and served before a meal. Choose thinly sliced cooked meats such as salami; ham and other smoked meats; a variety of cheeses, cubed or sliced; anchovy fillets and pickled or marinated vegetables. Arrange these separately on a lettuce-lined platter or on individual serving plates. Use Caponata (see above) or Marinated Antipasto Vegetables (see page 8) in the arrangement or pass separately along with breadsticks. Provide a good quality olive oil and red wine vinegar in cruets.

CREPES BOLOGNESE

"Make a main-dish soup in advance and you will have time to create these unique ham-filled crepes. Just add a salad and bread, if you wish."

1 c. chopped fresh parsley
⅓ c. grated **Parmesan** cheese
¼ c. vegetable oil
¼ c. sliced green onions
2 tbsp. butter or margarine
1 clove garlic, crushed
1 tsp. dried basil leaves, crushed
1 tsp. fresh lemon juice
4 drops hot pepper sauce

Preheat oven to 350° F. Grease a baking sheet. Place parsley, cheese, oil, green onions, butter or margarine, garlic, basil, lemon juice and hot pepper sauce in a blender container or food processor bowl; cover and blend or process until uniform. Set aside.

1 c. ground ham (about 4 oz.)
⅓ c. soft bread crumbs
¼ c. chopped celery
3 tbsp. dairy sour cream
2 tbsp. chopped walnuts
⅛ tsp. dried basil leaves, crushed
⅛ tsp. freshly ground pepper

In a small bowl, mix ham, bread crumbs, celery, sour cream, walnuts, basil and pepper until well blended.

continued on next page . . .

Crepes Bolognese continued...

8 crepes .... Spoon 2 tablespoons of the ham filling into center of
(see below) each crepe. Roll and place seam-side down on baking
sheet. Cover with foil and bake for 15 minutes or until
heated through.

Cherry tomatoes ... To serve, place crepes on individual serving plates.
(optional) Spoon 1 tablespoon of the parsley sauce over each
crepe. Garnish with optional cherry tomatoes.

Makes 8 servings

CREPES

2 c. milk .... In a small mixer bowl at low speed, beat milk, flour,
1 c. all-purpose flour eggs and salt until smooth. Cover and let stand at
3 eggs room temperature for 30 minutes.
½ tsp. salt

¼ c. real butter, ... Blend in melted butter. Heat a 7-inch skillet or crepe
melted pan over medium-high heat; coat with butter. Imme-
Additional real diately pour 2 tablespoons of the batter into skillet and
butter quickly tilt skillet in all directions to spread evenly.
Cook for about 1 minute on the first side; turn and
cook about 30 seconds on the other. Place crepe on
a plate; cover and keep warm. Continue with the
remaining batter, brushing pan lightly with butter
before frying each crepe.

Makes about 16

FREEZING CREPES

While in the process of making crepes, it is easy to double the batch
and freeze the excess for another time. Simply stack the cooled crepes
with double thicknesses of waxed paper between them. Seal the stack in a
freezer bag and store in the freezer for 2 to 4 months. To use, remove the
bag and lift out as many crepes as you need. Return the rest to the freezer.
Thaw crepes about 1 hour, covered, at room temperature and use as
your recipe directs.

CRAB COQUILLE

"In larger portions, this could be a meal in itself. Plan a light tossed salad and London Broil to follow this creamy treat."

2 tbsp. butter or margarine, melted
1½ c. soft bread crumbs
1 c. real mayonnaise
⅓ c. minced celery
¼ c. finely shredded Swiss cheese (1 oz.)
¼ c. dry sherry
1 tbsp. chopped parsley
1 clove garlic, minced
½ tsp. paprika
Pinch of white pepper

Lightly oil six ovenproof shells or individual shallow baking dishes. Set in a 15½ x 10½ x 1-inch jelly roll pan. In a small bowl, mix butter or margarine with ½ cup of the bread crumbs; set aside. In a medium bowl, mix remaining 1 cup crumbs, mayonnaise, celery, cheese, sherry, parsley, garlic, paprika and pepper until well blended.

2 pkg. (6 oz. ea.) frozen crab meat, thawed and drained

Cut crab meat into ½-inch pieces and stir into mayonnaise mixture. Lightly spoon into shells or baking dishes and sprinkle buttered crumbs on top. Broil 6 inches from heat source for 2 to 4 minutes or until golden brown and bubbly.

Fresh parsley sprigs

Garnish with parsley and serve immediately.

Makes 6 (about ⅓-cup) servings

USING FINGER BOWLS

Finger bowls are not often used in the home, and yet they are so appreciated after certain foods. Peeling shrimp, cracking crab or dipping artichoke leaves can create an untidy feeling. A refreshing finger bowl is a real treat. Place a small bowl on a doily-lined plate and fill it with lukewarm water. Add a wedge or slice of lemon or a drop of peppermint extract. Prepare a bowl for each guest and provide each with an extra napkin. Remove the bowls before the next course is served.

SOLE AND VEGETABLES JOANNE

"Definitely part of a gourmet dinner; get the freshest fish you can find."

2 sole fillets . . . . Lightly butter four individual ramekins. Pat fillets dry
   (4 oz. ea.) with paper towels. Cut each fillet in half crosswise;
1 c. dry white wine roll from cut side and fasten with a wooden pick.
½ c. diced carrots Place seam-side down in a cold 10-inch skillet. Add
¼ c. diced celery wine, carrots, celery, green onion, parsley, salt and
2 tbsp. sliced green pepper. Over medium heat, cover and bring to a boil;
   onion reduce heat to low and simmer for 6 minutes or
1 tbsp. minced fresh until fish barely flakes with a fork. With a slotted
   parsley spoon, remove fish and place in ramekins; keep
¼ tsp. salt warm. Remove vegetables from skillet; set aside.
⅛ tsp. freshly ground Reserve ¼ cup of the liquid and set aside; discard
   pepper remaining liquid.

2 tbsp. butter or . . . . . . Preheat oven to 350° F. Over medium heat, melt
   margarine butter or margarine in skillet. Return vegetables to
1 c. sliced fresh skillet, add mushrooms and sauté for 2 minutes. Stir
   mushrooms in flour. Cook and stir for 1 to 2 minutes. Add milk
1 tbsp. all-purpose and reserved liquid. Stirring, bring to a boil and
   flour boil until thickened.
¾ c. milk

Spoon about ½ cup of the sauce over each fillet. Bake for 5 minutes or until fish is heated through, but is not dry.

   Celery leaves . . . . Garnish with celery leaves. Serve immediately.

Makes 4 servings

NOTES:

TORTILLA SOUP

¼ c. chopped onion ... In a heavy 2-quart saucepan over medium heat,
1 tbsp. vegetable oil   sauté onion in oil for 5 minutes or until soft and
   or olive oil   golden. Add garlic; cook and stir for 1 minute.
1 clove garlic, minced Remove from heat.

1 can (16 oz.) .... Place tomatoes in a blender container; cover and
   whole tomatoes   blend until puréed. Add tomatoes, broth, vegetable
1 can (10½ oz.) con-   juice cocktail, water, picanté sauce, sugar, Worces-
   densed beef broth   tershire sauce, cumin and chili powder to onion mix-
¾ c. vegetable juice   ture. Return pan to heat and bring to a boil; reduce
   cocktail   heat to low and simmer, uncovered, for 15 minutes.
½ c. water
1 to 2 tbsp. picanté
   sauce
1 tsp. sugar
1 tsp. Worcestershire
   sauce
½ tsp. ground cumin
½ tsp. chili powder

2 corn tortillas, ... Cut tortillas into 1-inch strips, then into triangles.
   6" each   Stir into hot mixture and simmer for 10 minutes.

Dairy sour cream ...   To serve, ladle soup into small bowls or mugs. Top
   (about 3 tbsp.)   each serving with about ½ tablespoon sour cream.
                        Serve immediately.

Makes 6 (⅔-cup) servings

CHILLED AVOCADO SOUP

1 lg. avocado, ... Place avocado, broth or bouillon, half-and-half,
   pitted, peeled and   onion, lemon juice, salt and pepper in a blender
   cut up   container or food processor bowl; cover and blend
1 c. chicken broth   or process until very smooth. Cover and chill for 1 to
   or bouillon   2 hours.
1 c. half-and-half
1 tbsp. chopped onion
2 tsp. fresh lemon
   juice
½ tsp. salt
⅛ tsp. ground white
   pepper

Chopped tomato .... Garnish with tomato.

Makes 6 (½-cup) servings

ORIENTAL SOUP

3 c. water . . . . In a medium saucepan over high heat, bring water
5 tsp. chicken and bouillon to a boil. Add noodles, carrot and
   bouillon granules gingerroot; reduce heat to low and simmer for 3 to
½ c. uncooked fine 5 minutes or until noodles and carrots are barely tender.
   egg noodles
¼ c. thinly sliced
   carrot
¼ to ½ tsp. minced
   fresh gingerroot

⅓ c. frozen tiny . . . . Add shrimp and green onion; simmer for 2 minutes
   shrimp or until shrimp are heated through.
2 tbsp. thinly sliced
   green onion

¾ c. bite-size pieces . . . Add spinach; simmer for 1 minute or until spinach is
   fresh spinach tender. Serve immediately.

Makes 6 (½-cup) servings

LETTUCE AND PEA SOUP

2 c. ¼″ diced . . . . In a 3-quart saucepan over medium-high heat,
   French bread sauté bread cubes in butter or margarine until gold-
¼ c. butter or en brown and crisp; drain on paper towels and set
   margarine aside. Wipe crumbs from pan with paper towels.

⅓ c. chopped onion. . . . In the saucepan over medium-high heat, sauté
2 tsp. vegetable oil onion in oil for 1 minute or until onion is limp.

3 c. coarsely . . . . Add lettuce, broth, peas and pepper. Bring to a boil;
   chopped iceberg remove from heat and cool for 5 minutes. Place half
   lettuce at a time in a blender container; cover and blend at
3 cans (10¾ oz. ea.) high speed for 1 minute or until very smooth. Trans-
   condensed fer to a 2-quart bowl.
   chicken broth
2 pkg. (10 oz. ea.)
   frozen tiny peas
¼ tsp. ground white
   pepper

Serve immediately or chill and serve cold. Garnish
individual servings with bread cubes.

Makes 12 (½-cup) servings

CELERY VICTORIA

1 bunch celery . . . . — Trim off root end of celery but do not separate ribs. Remove coarse outer ribs, reserving some leaves for garnish. Rinse celery bunch. Cut crosswise so bottom section is 6 inches long. Reserve top portion for another use. Cut bottom section crosswise into six 1-inch portions. Securely tie the outside of each portion with string to hold it together. Place in a 12-inch skillet.

1 can (10½ oz.) . . . . — Add broth. Cover and bring to a boil over medium condensed beef heat; cook for 15 minutes or until crisp-tender. broth Remove celery with a slotted spoon and place in a shallow dish.

½ c. vegetable oil . . . . . — Place oil, vinegar, water, parsley, Italian herb season-
3 tbsp. cider vinegar ing, garlic, salt, curry powder and pepper in a blender
1 tbsp. water container; cover and blend until uniform. Pour over
1 tbsp. minced fresh celery. Cover and chill for 3 hours, turning celery
   parsley several times.
1 tsp. dried Italian
   herb seasoning,
   crushed
1 med. clove garlic,
   minced
½ tsp. salt
¼ tsp. curry powder
⅛ tsp. freshly ground
   pepper

1 whole pimiento, ... — To serve, drain celery and place on individual serv-
   cut in strips ing plates. Remove string and garnish with pimiento and celery leaves.

Makes 6 servings

chapter 2 CONTENTS

Dips and Spreads | *Page*

Pictured on the preceding page are Salmon Appetizer Ball and Herb Cheese Dip.

Dips and Spreads

HERB CHEESE DIP

1 pkg. (8 oz.) cream... In a small mixer bowl at medium speed, beat cheese,
  cheese, softened   yogurt or milk, parsley, onion, tarragon, salt and
¼ c. plain yogurt or   pepper until well blended. Cover and chill at least 30
  milk   minutes.
2 tbsp. minced fresh
  parsley
2 tbsp. minced onion
½ tsp. dried tarragon
  leaves, crushed
¼ tsp. salt
¼ tsp. freshly ground
  pepper

Milk............... To serve, thin with milk to desired consistency. Sprinkle
Chopped fresh   with parsley and serve with vegetables.
  parsley
Raw vegetables

Makes 1 cup

PREPARING RAW VEGETABLES FOR DIPS

Raw vegetables are popular with dips because they are low in calories and are not too filling. Dieters can even skip the dips and eat the crisp vegetables plain. Select a variety of vegetables that can be eaten raw; cut them into sticks, flowerets, diagonal slices or other decorative shapes. Crisp in a bowl of ice water, then drain. Wrap the vegetables individually in plastic wrap or seal in plastic bags and refrigerate for several hours. Just before serving, arrange them on a bed of crushed ice. You will need to drain off the water as the ice melts, or have a second batch of vegetables ready for a fresh bowl of ice.

CREAMY ITALIAN DIP

"The green peppers make pretty containers surrounded with raw vegetable dippers."

2 c. dairy sour cream . .	In a small mixer bowl at low speed, beat sour cream, salad dressing mix, butter or margarine, parsley and herb seasoning until well blended. Cover and chill at least 2 hours.
1 pkg. (1.18 oz.) dry creamy Italian salad dressing mix	
½ c. butter or margarine, melted	
1 tbsp. minced fresh parsley	
½ tsp. dried Italian herb seasoning	
2 lg. green peppers, . . . chilled	Remove tops and seeds from green peppers. If necessary, cut a thin slice off the bottoms so peppers will stand. Wrap and chill.
Paprika	To serve, spoon dip into peppers. Sprinkle with paprika. Serve with chips or vegetables.
Corn chips or raw vegetables	

Makes about 2¼ cups

AVOCADO DIP

"This tasty mixture keeps its color surprisingly well."

1 c. dairy sour . . . . cream	In a medium bowl, mix sour cream, avocado, chilies, lemon juice and garlic salt until well blended.
1 med. ripe avocado, pitted, peeled and mashed	
2 tbsp. chopped green chilies	
2 tsp. fresh lemon juice	
½ tsp. garlic salt	
6 slices bacon, ... fried crisp and drained	To serve, crumble bacon and fold into dip, sprinkling some bacon on top for garnish. Serve with chips.
Chips	

Makes 1½ cups

NEWBURG DIP

½ c. minced onion	In a medium saucepan over medium-high heat, sauté onion, celery and green pepper in butter or margarine for 3 minutes or until golden.
¼ c. minced celery	
¼ c. minced green pepper	
2 tbsp. butter or margarine	
¼ c. all-purpose flour	Stir in flour. Cook and stir over medium heat for 1 to 2 minutes. Add milk. Stirring, bring to a boil and boil until thickened.
2 c. milk	
2 egg yolks, lightly beaten	Gradually stir about one-third of the hot mixture into the egg yolks, then stir back into hot mixture in saucepan. Cook and stir over medium heat for 1 minute. Remove from heat.
1 pkg. (6 oz.) frozen crab meat, thawed, drained and chopped	Stir in crab meat, sherry, lemon juice, Worcestershire sauce, salt, paprika and red pepper. Cook and stir over low heat until heated through (do not boil).
¼ c. dry sherry	
1 tbsp. fresh lemon juice	
2 tsp. Worcestershire sauce	
1 tsp. salt	
½ tsp. paprika	
⅛ tsp. ground red pepper	
Chips	Pour into a chafing dish and serve warm with chips.

Makes 3 cups

21

DOUBLE R RANCH DIP

"Thin with milk to make a salad dressing."

1 c. real mayonnaise ..	In a small bowl, mix mayonnaise, buttermilk, garlic,
½ c. buttermilk	basil, salt and pepper until well blended. Cover and
¼ tsp. minced garlic	chill for 30 minutes.
¼ tsp. dried basil	
leaves, crushed	
⅛ tsp. salt	
⅛ tsp. freshly ground	
pepper	

Cauliflower or	Serve with vegetables.
broccoli flowerets,	
whole mushrooms	
and green pepper	
strips	

Makes about 1½ cups

SALSA DIP

3 lg. or 4 med.	Peel, seed, chop and drain tomatoes.
tomatoes	

1 can (4¼ oz.)	In a medium bowl, mix tomatoes, olives, chilies, green
chopped ripe olives	onion, vinegar, oil, salt and garlic powder. Cover and
1 can (4 oz.) diced	chill at least 1 hour.
green chilies*	
2 tbsp. chopped	
green onion	
1 tbsp. red wine	
vinegar	
1 tsp. olive or	
vegetable oil	
½ tsp. salt	
¼ tsp. garlic powder	

Tortilla or	To serve, drain well and place in a bowl. Serve with
corn chips	chips.

*"Hot" chilies may be used for a sharper flavor.

Makes about 2¼ cups

NOTES:

HOT TUNA DIP

1 pkg. (8 oz.) . . . . In a small saucepan, mix cheeses and chili sauce.
   cream cheese,   Cook and stir over low heat until smooth and hot.
   softened
1 jar (5 oz.) sharp pas-
   teurized process
   cheese spread
2 tbsp. chili sauce

1 can (6½ oz.) solid . . . Stir in tuna and green onion. Thin with milk to desired
   white tuna,   consistency.
   drained and flaked
2 tbsp. thinly sliced
   green onion
   Milk

   Ground red . . . . Pour into a chafing dish and garnish with a dash of
   pepper   red pepper. Serve warm with chips.
   Chips

Makes 2 cups

CHILI CON QUESO

"Set your fondue pot in front of the fireplace and enjoy this hot dip."

8 oz. Monterey . . . . In a small saucepan, mix cheeses and mayonnaise.
   Jack cheese,   Cook and stir over low heat until cheeses are
   shredded (2 c.)   melted (do not boil).
1 pkg. (3 oz.) cream
   cheese, cut in
   chunks
½ c. real mayonnaise

2 cans (4 oz. ea.) . . . . . Stir in chilies, onion and hot pepper sauce to taste.
   chopped green
   chilies, undrained
1 tbsp. minced onion
   Hot pepper sauce

   Corn or . . . . Pour into a chafing dish and serve warm with chips.
   tortilla chips

Makes about 1½ cups

NOTES:

BRAUNSCHWEIGER DIP

"A hearty dip that's good with beer. Try it with liverwurst, too."

5 oz. braunschweiger	In a small mixer bowl at low speed, beat braun-
1 c. dairy sour cream	schweiger until smooth. Add sour cream, soup mix
½ env. (about 3 tbsp.)	and Worcestershire sauce; beat well. Cover and chill
dry onion soup mix	at least 1 hour to develop flavor.
¼ tsp. Worcestershire	
sauce	
Fresh parsley	Garnish with parsley or egg. Serve with chips or crack-
sprigs or chopped	ers or use as a filling for Petits Choux (see page 68).
hard-cooked egg	
Corn chips	
or crackers	

Makes 1½ cups

AMBER GLOW

"The ingredients may sound strange, but try it with a glass of chilled chablis or rosé. You will need the wine if you use the larger amount of hot pepper flakes!"

1 pkg. (8 oz.)	Press cream cheese into an 8-ounce plastic marga-
cream cheese,	rine tub or a small bowl. Loosen edges with a spatula
softened	and invert onto the center of a shallow serving dish.
	Smooth surface with a spatula.
1 jar (10 oz.) apricot . . .	In a small bowl, mix preserves, mustard, horseradish
preserves (¾ c.)	and hot pepper flakes or sauce until well blended.
1½ tsp. dry mustard	Pour over cheese.
1 tsp. prepared	
horseradish	
⅛ to ¼ tsp. hot pepper	
flakes, crushed,	
or hot pepper	
sauce	
¼ c. chopped salted . . .	Sprinkle with nuts. Serve with crackers.
peanuts	
Crackers	

Makes ¾ cup sauce

NOTES:

MINT DIP

"Arrange the fruit to be dipped in a pineapple shell or scooped out melon half for a summer party."

1 pkg. (3 oz.) cream... In a medium bowl, beat
cheese, softened cream cheese and sour
⅓ c. dairy sour cream cream until smooth.

1 tbsp. brown sugar... Stir in brown sugar, mint
1 tsp. dried mint flakes, optional creme de
flakes, crushed* menthe, mint extract and
1 tsp. green creme optional green food color.
de menthe Cover and chill for 30 to
(optional) 40 minutes.
3 drops mint extract*
1 or 2 drops green
food color
(optional)

Apple slices,........ To serve, place dip in a
grapes, pineapple small bowl on a plate;
chunks and pear surround with fruit.
slices

*2 tablespoons minced fresh mint leaves may be substituted for dried mint and mint extract.

Makes ¾ cup

HONEY 'N' SPICE DIP

"Make this serve-yourself fruit cocktail for an informal dinner."

1½ c. cottage cheese ... Place cottage cheese,
3 tbsp. honey honey, lemon juice and
2 tsp. fresh lemon cinnamon in a food proc-
juice essor bowl or blender con-
¼ tsp. ground tainer; cover and process
cinnamon or blend until smooth.
Spoon into a small bowl.

½ c. plain yogurt ...... Fold in yogurt. Cover and
chill.

Ground cinnamon.. To serve, sprinkle with
Assorted fresh fruit cinnamon and serve with
fruit.

Makes about 1½ cups

DILL VEGETABLE DIP

"Also good with fish balls or shrimp."

½ c. real mayonnaise..   In a small bowl, mix mayonnaise, sour cream, pars-
½ c. dairy sour cream   ley, onion, dill weed and celery salt until smooth.
2 tbsp. minced fresh   Cover and chill at least 30 minutes.
    parsley
2 tsp. grated onion
1 tsp. dried dill weed,
    crushed
½ tsp. celery salt

   Raw vegetables . . . . .   Serve with vegetables.

Makes 1 cup

FLORENTINE DIP

"A pleasing blend of flavors with a fresh, green color."

½ c. chopped onion . . .   In a small skillet over medium-high heat, sauté onion
1 med. clove garlic,   and garlic in butter or margarine for 3 minutes or
    minced   until just beginning to brown.
2 tbsp. butter or
    margarine

1 pkg. (10 oz.) . . . .   Place in a blender container or food processor bowl
    frozen chopped   with spinach, cream cheese, lemon juice, mustard,
    spinach, cooked   salt, pepper, hot pepper sauce and nutmeg; cover
    and well drained   and blend or process until uniform. Cover and chill at
1 pkg. (3 oz.) cream   least 1 hour.
    cheese, softened
2 tsp. fresh lemon
    juice
½ tsp. Dijon mustard
¼ tsp. salt
¼ tsp. freshly ground
    pepper
6 drops hot pepper
    sauce
   Dash of ground
    nutmeg

   Milk . . . .   To serve, thin with milk to desired consistency. Serve
   Chips   with chips.

Makes 1¼ cups

CRIPPLE CREEK CHEESE SPREAD

¼ c. butter or .... In a small saucepan, mix butter or margarine, beef
    margarine   bouillon and paprika. Cook and stir over low heat until
1 tbsp. beef bouillon   butter or margarine is melted and bouillon is dis-
    granules   solved. Remove from heat; set aside to cool slightly.
1 tsp. paprika

1 c. small curd .... Place cheeses and hot pepper sauce in a food proces-
    cottage cheese   sor bowl or blender container; cover and process or
    (about 8 oz.)   blend until smooth. With motor running, gradually pour
4 oz. cream cheese,   in butter mixture and blend well. Pack into a crock.
    softened   Cover and chill.
2 oz. blue cheese,
    crumbled
4 drops hot pepper
    sauce

    Water biscuits ...... Serve with biscuits or crackers.
    or unsalted
    crackers

Makes 2 cups

GOUDA HERB SPREAD

"Look for a large Gouda in the deli or cheese shop."

1 whole (14 oz.) ...... Cut top from cheese with a decorative design. With a
    Gouda cheese   spoon carefully scoop out cheese, leaving a thin
                 shell. Set shell aside. Finely shred cheese.

1 pkg. (3 oz.) cream... In a small mixer bowl at low speed, beat cheeses, milk
    cheese, softened   or half-and-half, sage and onion salt until well
½ c. milk or   blended. (Mixture will not be smooth.) Pack into
    half-and-half   Gouda shell. Cover and chill.
1 tsp. ground sage
1 tsp. onion salt

    Rye or whole .... Serve with crackers.
    wheat crackers

Makes about 1¾ cups

NOTES:

MEDITERRANEAN SPREAD

¼ c. peanuts . . . . Place nuts in a food processor bowl; cover and process until finely ground.

1 can (15½ oz.) . . . . Add beans, reserved liquid, lemon juice, oil,
  garbanzo beans, garlic, salt and pepper. Cover and process until mix-
  drained, and 3 tbsp. ture is uniform and well blended. Taste for additional
  liquid reserved seasoning.
2 tbsp. fresh lemon
  juice
1 tbsp. peanut or
  olive oil
3 med. cloves garlic,
  crushed
⅛ tsp. salt
  Dash of freshly
  ground pepper

1 tbsp. minced . . . . Cover and chill or serve immediately. Sprinkle with
  fresh parsley parsley. Serve with pita bread or crackers.
  Whole wheat pita
  bread, cut in
  triangles, or
  sesame crackers

Makes 1½ cups

SHERRIED CHEESE SPREAD

"Make this classic spread for gift-giving. It is easy to make and keeps well."

1 c. butter or . . . . In a small mixer bowl at medium speed, beat butter
  margarine, softened or margarine until fluffy. Gradually beat in cheese,
10 oz. sharp Cheddar scraping bowl occasionally. Add sherry, horseradish,
  cheese, finely garlic powder and hot pepper sauce; beat well.
  shredded (2½ c.) Pack into a crock or covered container. Cover and
¼ c. dry sherry chill at least 24 hours.
1 tbsp. prepared
  horseradish
⅛ tsp. garlic powder
  Dash of hot pepper
  sauce

Crackers . . . . Remove from refrigerator about 1 hour before serving
  with crackers.

Makes 2⅔ cups

DEVILED EGG SPREAD

6 hard-cooked eggs,.. finely chopped
½ c. minced celery
3 tbsp. real mayonnaise
1½ tsp. prepared mustard
¾ tsp. onion salt
¼ tsp. freshly ground pepper
¼ tsp. dried oregano leaves, crushed

In a small bowl, mix eggs, celery, mayonnaise, mustard, onion salt, pepper and oregano until well blended. Mound on a serving dish and shape as desired. Smooth with a spatula. Cover and chill for 2 hours.

1 pkg. (3 oz.) cream... cheese, softened
1½ tbsp. milk
Pimiento-stuffed olives, sliced
Paprika
Cocktail bread or Melba toast

In a small bowl, beat cream cheese and milk until smooth. Spread mixture on top and sides of egg mixture. Garnish with olives and a sprinkling of paprika. Serve with bread or toast.

Makes 1½ cups

CHILI CHEESE SPREAD

"If you'd rather use this as a dip, add milk to thin it to dipping consistency."

1 pkg. (8 oz.) cream... cheese, softened
3 tbsp. chopped fresh parsley
2 tbsp. minced green pepper
2 tbsp. grated onion
2 tsp. chili powder
½ tsp. salt

In a medium bowl, mix cream cheese, parsley, green pepper, onion, chili powder and salt until well blended.

1 lg. green pepper .... (optional)

Remove top and seeds from optional green pepper. If necessary, cut a thin slice off the bottom of pepper so it will stand. Pack cheese mixture into green pepper shell or into a crock. Cover and chill.

Crackers .... Serve with crackers.

Makes about 1¼ cups

NOTES:

29

RADISH SPREAD

"Your guests may have a hard time identifying the ingredients in this buttery spread."

1 pkg. (3 oz.) cream...   In a small bowl, mix cheese, butter or margarine,
   cheese, softened   mustard, garlic, salt and pepper until well blended.
2 tbsp. butter or
   margarine,
   softened
1 tsp. prepared
   mustard
1 med. clove garlic,
   crushed and
   minced
¼ tsp. salt
⅛ tsp. freshly ground
   pepper

½ c. finely shredded ...   Stir in radishes and parsley. Cover and chill at least
   red radishes   1 hour.
   (about 1 bunch)
2 tbsp. chopped fresh
   parsley

   Melba toast, ...   Serve with toast, crackers or vegetables.
   crackers or
   raw vegetables

Makes about 1 cup

DELPHI SPREAD

1 pkg. (8 oz.) cream...   In a small mixer bowl at low speed, beat cheeses for 3
   cheese, softened   minutes.
8 oz. sharp Cheddar
   cheese, finely
   shredded (2 c.)

1 can (4½ oz.) ....   Stir in olives, nuts, parsley, lemon pepper and hot
   chopped ripe olives   pepper sauce. Cover and chill for 2 hours.
½ c. finely chopped
   walnuts
1 tbsp. minced fresh
   parsley
½ tsp. lemon pepper
¼ tsp. hot pepper
   sauce

continued on next page . . .

Delphi Spread continued...

Whole pimiento, ...	On a sheet of waxed paper, form cheese mixture
drained	into two 3-inch balls. Cut whole pimiento into small
Crackers	decorative shapes and decorate as desired. Serve
	with crackers.

Makes 2 (3-inch) balls

SHRIMP SPREAD

½ **c. real mayonnaise** ..	In a small bowl, mix mayonnaise, cream cheese,
1 **pkg. (3 oz.) cream**	lemon juice, salt, pepper and hot pepper sauce until
cheese, softened	smooth.
1 **tsp. fresh lemon**	
juice	
⅛ **tsp. salt**	
⅛ **tsp. freshly ground**	
pepper	
5 **drops hot pepper**	
sauce	
1 **pkg. (6 oz.) frozen** ..	Stir in shrimp, celery, green pepper and onion. Cover
cooked shrimp,	and chill.
thawed, drained	
and finely chopped	
1 **tbsp. minced celery**	
1 **tbsp. minced green**	
pepper	
1 **tbsp. minced onion**	
Crackers or	Serve with crackers or toast.
toast rounds	

Makes 1½ cups

STORING DIPS AND SPREADS

Dips and spreads should usually be made several hours before serving. This gives the flavor a chance to develop properly and allows the mixture to become well chilled. A firm spread may need to come to room temperature again for the desired softness, but most dips are best served cold. Store cheese spreads, tightly wrapped, in the refrigerator; some freeze well, but this is not usually necessary unless you have a large quantity. Do not freeze dips containing mayonnaise, sour cream, gelatin or hard-cooked egg whites.

SAUSALITO SPREAD

"A showy spread for a cocktail buffet. Make the base the day before and garnish just before serving."

1 pkg. (8 oz.) cream... Line the bottom of an 8 x 1½-inch round cake pan
cheese with chives, with waxed paper. In a small mixer bowl at high speed,
softened* beat cream cheese until smooth. Add Muenster, sour
8 oz. Muenster cheese, cream, Worcestershire sauce, onion and garlic pow-
shredded ders and pepper. Beat about 5 minutes or until fluffy.
½ c. dairy sour cream (Some small chunks of Muenster will remain.)
1 tsp. Worcestershire Spread cheese mixture into pan. Cover and chill at
sauce least 2 hours.
½ tsp. onion powder
¼ tsp. garlic powder
¼ tsp. freshly ground
pepper

1 hard-cooked egg, ... Unmold cheese mixture onto a chilled serving plate.
minced, or 1 jar Carefully peel off waxed paper. Smooth surface with
(2 oz.) caviar a spatula. Place egg or caviar in center. Surround
Sliced ripe olives with a ring of olive slices. Drain shrimp well and
1 pkg. (6 oz.) frozen cut in half, if large. Place a ring of shrimp around the
shrimp, thawed, or outer edge. Stand cucumbers around sides of
1 c. sm. cooked cheese round. Lay a row of cucumbers on the plate
fresh shrimp to form a scalloped edge. Serve with crackers.
12 thin slices
cucumber, cut in
half
Crackers

*Or use 1 package (8 ounces) cream cheese and 1 tablespoon minced chives.

Make 1 (8-inch) round

HAM AND CHICKEN PATÉ

"Freeze your leftover chicken and combine it with the remnants of the holiday ham."

1½ c. cubed cooked .... chicken 1 c. cubed cooked ham	Place chicken and ham in a food processor bowl; cover and process until minced, about 8 seconds.
⅓ c. butter or mar- .... garine, softened ½ tsp. dried thyme leaves, crushed ¼ tsp. ground marjoram ¼ tsp. salt Dash of freshly ground pepper	Add butter or margarine, thyme, marjoram, salt and pepper. Process until well blended, about 3 seconds. Taste for additional salt and pepper.
1 or 2 bay leaves...... (optional)	Place optional bay leaf in bottom of a small crock or glass jar. Spoon in mixture and smooth top. Cover and chill.
Crackers or......... cocktail bread	Remove from refrigerator about 30 minutes before serving with crackers or bread.

Makes about 1½ cups

CHICKEN LIVER PATÉ

½ lb. chicken livers .... 1 med. onion, chopped ¼ c. butter or margarine	In a small skillet over medium heat, sauté livers and onion in butter or margarine for 5 minutes or until livers are cooked through.
¼ tsp. salt .... ¼ tsp. freshly ground pepper	Place liver mixture, salt and pepper in a blender container or food processor bowl; cover and blend or process just until smooth. Transfer to a small bowl. Cover and chill for 30 minutes.
2 hard-cooked........ eggs, minced 1 tbsp. minced fresh parsley 1 tbsp. cognac Lettuce leaves Assorted crackers	Stir in eggs, parsley and cognac. Mound on a bed of lettuce. Serve with crackers.

Makes 1½ cups

TUNA-NUT PATÉ

1 can (7 oz.) chunk white tuna, drained	Lightly oil a 1½-cup bowl. In a small mixer bowl at low speed, beat tuna and cream cheese just until blended.
4 oz. cream cheese, softened	
¼ c. finely chopped nuts	Beat in nuts, olives, onion, mustard, thyme, salt and hot pepper sauce. Pack firmly into bowl. Cover and chill at least 2 hours.
2 tbsp. finely chopped pimiento-stuffed olives	
1 tbsp. grated onion	
½ tsp. dry mustard	
¼ tsp. dried thyme leaves, crushed	
¼ tsp. salt	
¼ tsp. hot pepper sauce	
Fresh parsley sprigs Assorted crackers	To serve, loosen edges with a spatula and unmold onto a serving dish. Smooth surface with a spatula. Garnish with parsley. Serve with crackers.

Makes 1½ cups

CHEDDAR-NUT PATÉ

"Make this at the last minute, or pack it away in pretty containers for gift-giving or entertaining."

8 oz. sharp Cheddar cheese, shredded (2 c.)	In a small mixer bowl at medium speed, beat cheese, butter or margarine and wine until well blended and fluffy.
¾ c. butter or margarine, softened	
3 tbsp. tawny port wine	
½ c. chopped walnuts	At low speed, beat in nuts. Pack into a crock or a glass jar. Cover and chill.
Crackers and fresh fruit	Remove from refrigerator about 1 hour before serving with crackers and fruit.

Makes about 1¾ cups

NOTES:

FROSTED PARTY LOG

8 oz. cooked ham, ... Place ham and onion in a
   cubed   blender container or food
¼ c. chopped onion   processor bowl; cover
                           and blend or process
                           until minced. Transfer to
                           a small bowl.

⅓ c. real mayonnaise.. Add mayonnaise, raisins
3 tbsp. raisins   and curry; mix well. On a
½ tsp. curry powder   sheet of waxed paper,
                           form into a 9-inch log.
                           Wrap and chill at least 1
                           hour.

1 pkg. (3 oz.) cream... In a small bowl, beat
   cheese, softened   cream cheese and milk until smooth. Remove wrap
1 tbsp. milk   from log and place on a cutting board or platter. Frost
                           top and sides with cream cheese mixture.

   Celery leaves .... Decorate with celery leaves and tomato. Serve
   Cherry tomato   with crackers.
   Crackers

Makes 1 (9-inch) log

HOT PEPPER LOG

8 oz. sharp pasteur-... In a small mixer bowl at medium speed, beat cheeses
   ized process   and butter or margarine until uniform.
   American cheese,
   shredded (2 c.)
1 pkg. (3 oz.) cream
   cheese, softened
1 tbsp. butter or
   margarine

1 tbsp. chopped ...... Add green pepper, red pepper or pimiento and
   green pepper   pepper flakes; beat well. On a sheet of waxed paper,
1 tbsp. chopped red   form into a 7-inch log. Wrap and chill at least 3 hours.
   pepper or pimiento
¼ tsp. red pepper
   flakes, finely
   crushed

   Assorted crackers... Remove from refrigerator about 30 minutes before
                           serving. Remove wrap. Slice and serve with crackers.

Makes 1 (7-inch) log

35

BACON-CHEESE LOG

"Garnish this like a party favor with green onion brushes at each end."

4 oz. sharp .... Cheddar cheese, finely shredded (about 1 c.) 1 pkg. (3 oz.) cream cheese, softened	In a small mixer bowl at low speed, beat cheeses for 3 minutes.
6 slices bacon, ... fried crisp and crumbled 2 tbsp. minced green onion ⅛ tsp. ground red pepper (optional)	Add bacon, green onion and optional red pepper. Beat until well blended. Cover and chill at least 2 hours.
Green onion .... brushes (see page 65) Pimiento-stuffed olives Assorted crackers	On a sheet of waxed paper, form into a 6-inch log. Remove wrap. Place on a cheese board or serving plate. Garnish with green onions and olives. Serve with crackers.

Makes 1 (6-inch) log

PACKAGING GIFT SPREADS

Most cheese spreads keep very well in the refrigerator and make excellent gifts. Collect a variety of refrigerator containers for this purpose, such as margarine tubs, peanut butter jars, small shortening cans with plastic lids and ½-pint canning jars. Logs and balls should be securely wrapped in moisture- or vapor-proof wrap to prevent drying out. Aluminum foil is a good choice. Use your imagination to decorate the outside for an attractive gift.

ROSY SHRIMP MOLD

1 env. unflavored ..... gelatin 1 can (6 oz.) tomato juice	Lightly oil a 4-cup mold. In a medium saucepan, mix gelatin and tomato juice; let stand for 1 minute.

continued on next page . . .

Rosy Shrimp Mold continued...

1 **pkg. (8 oz.) cream** **cheese, softened** ¾ **c. real mayonnaise**	Add cream cheese and mayonnaise. Stir over low heat until gelatin is dissolved and the mixture is smooth. Remove from heat.
2 **cans (4½ oz. ea.)** **broken shrimp,** **drained** ¼ **c. finely chopped** **celery** 2 **tbsp. catsup** 1 **tbsp. minced green** **onion** 1 **tsp. prepared** **horseradish**	Stir in shrimp, celery, catsup, green onion and horse-radish. Pour into the mold. Cover and chill at least 4 hours or overnight.
Lemon slices **Watercress or fresh** **parsley sprigs** **Assorted crackers**	To serve, unmold onto a chilled plate. Garnish with lemon and watercress or parsley. Serve with crackers.

Makes 4 cups

HANDLING GELATIN MOLDS

Molded mixtures containing the right amount of gelatin can be unmolded an hour or more before serving time and safely stored in the refrigerator. To unmold, run a sharp knife around the top edge of the gelatin mixture. Dip the mold in comfortably hot water for 5 to 10 seconds (do not allow the edges to get too soft). Remove the mold to a towel and dry the outside. Cover the mold with a larger serving plate and invert. Shake or tap to release the contents. If this doesn't work, repeat the process. If all other efforts fail, insert a thin knife along the outer edge to the bottom of the mold to let in some air. This usually works.

ROQUEFORT CHEESE BALL

4 oz. cream cheese,... In a small mixer bowl at
  softened   low speed, beat cheeses
2 oz. Roquefort or blue for 2 minutes. Add green
  cheese, crumbled onion, optional wine or
2 oz. finely shredded vermouth and mustard.
  sharp Cheddar   Beat at medium speed
  cheese (½ c.)   for 3 minutes or until
1 tbsp. minced green   fluffy. Cover and chill for
  onion   2 hours.
1 tbsp. dry white wine
  or dry vermouth
  (optional)
¼ tsp. dry mustard

½ c. finely .... With wet hands shape
  chopped walnuts   into a 3-inch ball and roll
Fresh parsley sprigs in nuts. Place on a cheese
Assorted crackers   board or serving plate;
                         garnish with parsley. Serve
                         with crackers.

Makes 1 (3-inch) ball

SALMON APPETIZER BALL

1 pkg. (8 oz.) cream... In a small mixer bowl at medium speed, beat cream
  cheese, softened   cheese, lemon juice, onion, horseradish and liquid
1 tbsp. fresh lemon   smoke until well mixed.
  juice
1 tbsp. finely chopped
  onion
1 tsp. prepared
  horseradish
¼ tsp. liquid smoke

1 can (15½ oz.) .... Drain and flake salmon, remove any skin and bone.
  red salmon   At low speed, beat into cheese mixture until well
                         blended. Chill until firm enough to handle. Shape into
                         one large or two small mounds with wet hands. Place
                         on serving plate(s).

2 to 3 tbsp. minced ... Pat surface with parsley and nuts. Cover and chill.
  fresh parsley
¼ c. chopped pecans

Crackers .... Serve with crackers.

Makes 1 large or 2 small balls

chapter 3 CONTENTS

Hot Hors d'Oeuvres   *Page*

Pictured on the preceding page is Mexican Meatballs.

Hot Hors d'Oeuvres

MEXICAN MEATBALLS

"There's a surprise inside every meatball... a stuffed green olive."

1 lb. ground beef . . . . . ¼ c. grated raw potato 1 egg, lightly beaten 1½ tsp. chili powder 1 tsp. salt ¼ tsp. freshly ground pepper	In a medium bowl, mix beef, potato, egg, chili powder, salt and pepper until well blended.
40 sm. pimiento-. . . . . . . stuffed green olives	Shape ½ tablespoon of the meat mixture around each olive to make a ball. Place half of the meatballs in a large skillet over medium-high heat; sauté just until browned. Drain off fat; remove meatballs and keep warm. Repeat with remaining meatballs. Return all meatballs to skillet.
1 can (10 oz.) mild . . . . enchilada sauce 1 can (8 oz.) tomato sauce ½ c. beer ½ c. chopped green pepper ½ c. chopped onion 1 tbsp. brown sugar Pickled tiny corn cobs (optional)	In a small bowl, mix sauces, beer, green pepper, onion and brown sugar. Pour over meatballs. Over medium-high heat, bring sauce to a boil; reduce heat to low and simmer, uncovered, stirring occasionally, for 20 minutes or until sauce is thickened. Add corn cobs, if desired, and heat through.

To serve, place meatballs and sauce in a chafing dish; serve with wooden picks.

Makes about 40

WATER CHESTNUT MEATBALLS

½ lb. lean ground beef	Preheat oven to 375° F. In a medium bowl, mix beef, sausage, bread crumbs, water chestnuts, milk, soy
½ lb. bulk pork sausage	sauce, garlic salt and onion powder until well blend-
2 c. soft bread crumbs	ed. Form rounded teaspoonfuls into small balls.
1 can (8 oz.) water chestnuts, drained and chopped	Place in a 15½ x 10½ x 1-inch jelly roll pan. Bake for 8 minutes; gently turn each ball with a metal spatula and bake 10 to 12 minutes longer or until
¼ c. milk	well browned.
1 tbsp. soy sauce	
½ tsp. garlic salt	
¼ tsp. onion powder	

To serve, place meatballs in a chafing dish and serve hot. Do not cover. Serve with wooden picks.

Makes about 60

SPICY BARBECUE RIBS

"You will need to provide plates for these... and cloth napkins work better than paper for these finger-lickin' ribs."

2 lb. pork backribs or spareribs	Use a sharp heavy knife to cut ribs into 1-rib portions (or ask your butcher to cut them for you). Place ribs in
Cold water	a deep 4-quart kettle and cover with cold water. Over high heat, bring to a boil; reduce heat to low, cover and simmer for 1 hour or until tender. Drain; cover and and chill until about 1 hour before serving.
1 c. tomato juice	Preheat oven to 350° F. In a small saucepan, stir toge-
⅓ c. firmly packed brown sugar	ther tomato juice, brown sugar, chili sauce, vinegar, onion, Worcestershire sauce, chili powder, mustard,
¼ c. chili sauce	salt and pepper. Over high heat, bring to a boil;
¼ c. cider vinegar	reduce heat to low and simmer, covered, for 5
¼ c. minced onion	minutes.
2 tbsp. Worcestershire sauce	Place ribs in a 13 x 9 x 2-inch baking dish and spoon
2 tsp. chili powder	hot sauce over top. Bake for 30 minutes, turning and
1 tsp. dry mustard	brushing several times to coat ribs.
½ tsp. salt	
¼ tsp. freshly ground pepper	

To serve, place ribs and sauce in a chafing dish. Provide plenty of napkins.

Makes about 15 servings

STUFFED ROMAINE LEAVES

12 romaine leaves ..... In a large saucepan over medium heat, blanch romaine leaves, three to four at a time, in boiling water for 5 minutes or until very wilted. Drain well on paper towels; set aside.

1 jar (15 oz.) .... Pour sauce into a large
marinara sauce skillet; set aside.

⅓ c. minced onion .... In a medium skillet over
2 tbsp. butter or medium-high heat, sauté
margarine onion in butter or marga-
3 tbsp. all-purpose rine until soft. Stir in flour, salt and dill weed. Cook and
flour stir over medium heat for 1 to 2 minutes. Add milk.
¼ tsp. salt Stirring, bring to a boil and boil until very thick. Remove
⅛ tsp. dried dill weed, from heat.
crushed
¼ c. milk

2 eggs .... In a small mixer bowl at medium speed, beat eggs
1 pkg. (10 oz.) frozen well. Beat in hot onion sauce. Stir in spinach, cracker
chopped spinach, crumbs and cheese. Place 2 tablespoons of the
cooked and well spinach mixture into the center of each romaine
drained leaf. Fold sides over filling and roll up. Place seam-
¼ c. cracker crumbs side down in sauce in large skillet. Repeat with re-
3 tbsp. grated maining leaves. Place skillet over medium heat;
Parmesan cheese cover and simmer, basting rolls occasionally, for 15
to 20 minutes or until a knife inserted in center of roll
comes out clean.

To serve, cut each roll in half if desired. Place in chafing dish with sauce. Serve hot.

Makes 24

DEVILED DRUMETTES

12 chicken wings ...... (1) With a sharp knife, cut off wing tips (reserve for
(about 2¼ lb.) another use); cut each wing in half at the joint. (2) Push
the meat on the larger wing bone towards the larger
meatier section, trimming around the bone to cut the
meat free. (3) On the thinner wing bone, cut the meat
free starting at the less meaty end and push to the
meatier end, removing the smaller bone. (4) Wrap
skin around joint forming a "drumstick."

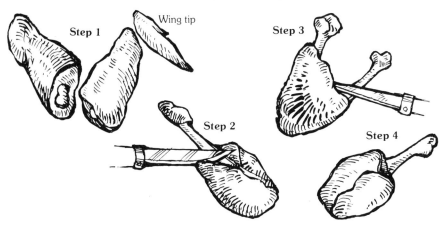

2 tbsp. vegetable oil .. In a heavy 10-inch skillet over high heat, cook
6 green onions, sliced chicken pieces in oil, turning frequently with tongs for
about 7 minutes or until evenly browned. Add green
onions, stir and reduce heat to low.

¾ c. water .... In a medium bowl, mix water, chili sauce, mustard,
⅓ c. chili sauce pineapple juice concentrate, vinegar, ginger and salt
⅓ c. Dijon mustard until blended. Pour over chicken and onions; cover
⅓ c. frozen pineapple and simmer for 20 minutes, stirring occasionally.
juice concentrate, Remove lid and continue cooking for 8 to 10 minutes
thawed or until meat is tender and sauce is slightly thickened.
3 tbsp. red wine Cool; cover and chill.
vinegar
¾ tsp. ground ginger
¾ tsp. salt

Additional .... About 30 minutes before serving, return chicken and
Sliced green sauce to skillet; cover and simmer over low heat until
onions (optional) heated through. Transfer to a chafing dish and serve
hot. Sprinkle with green onions if desired. Serve with
small plates and napkins.

Makes 24

SERVING FROM A CHAFING DISH

This versatile piece of equipment serves many purposes, but for hot hors d'oeuvres I use it strictly as a warming device. Make sure the food is at serving temperature before adding it to the pan. Pour boiling water into the water-bath pan and set the pan with the food over it. Adjust the flame to keep the water simmering. The water controls the temperature of the food so it will neither burn nor become cold. It usually takes quite a while for the water to evaporate, but you should check it from time to time and add more if needed.

BRIE IN CHAFING DISH

1 whole (8 oz.) .... **Brie cheese**	If desired, carefully remove coating from top surface of cheese. Place cheese in an 8- or 9-inch chafing
½ c. toasted almonds or pecans	dish. Sprinkle nuts over the top. Set over simmering water.
Water biscuits or .... unsalted crackers	As cheese melts, scrape up with crackers.

Makes 4 servings

NACHOS

1 can (8¼ oz.) .... **refried beans**
1 can (4 oz.) diced green chilies, drained
½ to 1 tsp. chili powder

Preheat oven to 350° F. In a 1½-cup heatproof bowl, mix beans, 2 tablespoons green chilies and chili powder. Place bowl in the middle of an ungreased 10-inch pie plate.

1 pkg. (8 oz.) .... **tortilla chips**
2 c. shredded Monterey Jack cheese (8 oz.)
Chopped tomato

Place one-half to two-thirds of the chips in the pie plate around beans. Sprinkle chips with remaining chilies and cheese. Bake for 10 to 15 minutes or until cheese is melted and beans are heated through.

Garnish beans with tomato. Serve remaining chips separately.

Makes 8 servings

PORK SPRING ROLLS WITH SWEET AND SOUR SAUCE

1 c. all-purpose .... In a small bowl, mix flour and water until smooth. Heat
    flour   an 8-inch nonstick skillet over low heat. With a soft
1 c. water   bristle brush, paint a thin layer of batter over bottom of
                       skillet, repeating several times to fill in spaces, using
about 2 tablespoons of the batter per wrapper. Cook about 2 minutes or until
edges curl away from edge of pan. Peel wrapper from pan; stack between
layers of waxed paper. Repeat until all batter is used; set wrappers aside.*

½ lb. ground pork ..... In a medium skillet over medium-high heat, sauté
3 tbsp. chopped water   pork, water chestnuts, carrot, green onion, gingerroot
    chestnuts   and garlic for 3 to 4 minutes or until pork is browned.
2 tbsp. shredded   Reduce heat to medium.
    carrot
1 green onion, minced
1 tsp. minced fresh
    gingerroot
1 clove garlic, minced

1 tbsp. cornstarch .... In a cup or small bowl, mix cornstarch, soy sauce and
1 tbsp. soy sauce   sherry until smooth; stir into pork mixture. Cook and
1 tbsp. dry sherry   stir until thickened. Remove from heat.

1 egg, lightly beaten... Stir egg into pork mixture.

Vegetable oil........ Pour vegetable oil into a large wok or skillet to a depth
                       of 1 inch. Heat oil over medium-high heat to about
375° F. Place 1 tablespoon of the pork filling in center of each wrapper. Moisten
edges with water. Fold bottom edge over filling; fold both sides of wrapper over
filling. Then roll enclosed filling in rest of wrapper. Place spring roll, seam-
side down, on waxed paper until ready to fry. Fry two or three spring rolls at
a time for 3 to 4 minutes, turning to brown on all sides. Remove and drain on
paper towels. Keep warm in oven until ready to serve.**

continued on next page . . .

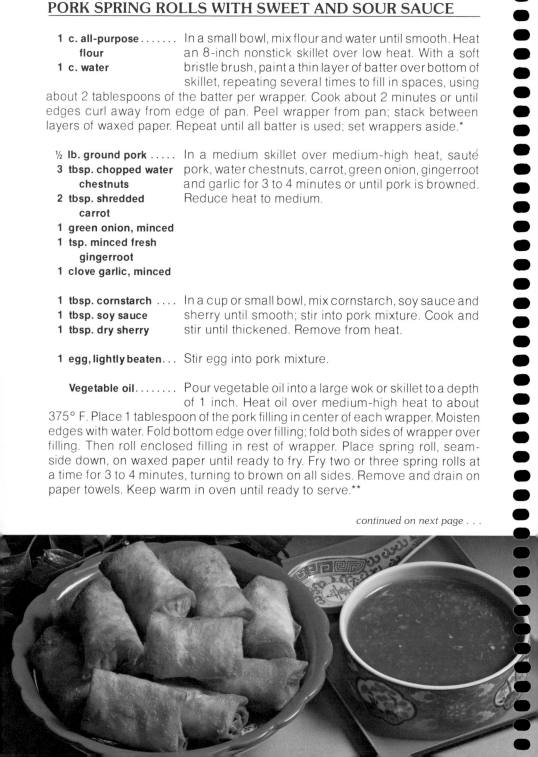

Pork Spring Rolls continued...

¾ c. water . . . . In a small saucepan, mix water, brown sugar, vinegar,
⅓ c. firmly packed cornstarch, soy sauce, sherry, gingerroot and garlic
   brown sugar until well blended. Over medium heat, bring to a boil;
¼ c. vinegar reduce heat to low and simmer, stirring, for 5 minutes
1 tbsp. cornstarch or until thickened.
1 tbsp. soy sauce
1 tbsp. dry sherry To serve, cut spring rolls in half if desired. Serve with
2 tsp. minced fresh sauce.
   gingerroot
2 tsp. minced garlic *Wrappers may be purchased already made if
   desired.

   **Spring rolls can be covered and frozen in a single
   layer. Reheat, uncovered, on an ungreased baking
   sheet in a preheated 350° F. oven for 20 minutes.

Makes about 36

MINI CORN DOGS

"Everyone cooks for themselves. These hearty little dogs are good with beer."

1 c. all-purpose flour . . In a small bowl, stir together flour, cornmeal, baking
3 tbsp. yellow powder and salt. With a pastry blender or two knives,
   cornmeal cut in butter or margarine until mixture resembles
1½ tsp. baking powder coarse crumbs.
½ tsp. salt
3 tbsp. butter or
   margarine

⅔ c. milk . . . . Beat in milk and egg until well blended. (Batter will be
1 egg, lightly beaten quite thick.)

3 c. vegetable oil . . . . . In a heavy medium saucepan, heat oil to 375° F. Carefully pour hot oil into a fondue pot and place over
   fondue burner.

Catsup . . . . Place catsup, mustard and relish in small serving
Prepared mustard bowls. Spear frankfurter pieces with fondue forks and
Pickle relish dip into batter, letting excess drip off. Fry, a few at a
1 pkg. (16 oz.) frank- time, in hot oil for about 2 minutes or until golden
   furters, cut in brown. Dip in catsup, mustard or relish.
   1" pieces

Makes 40 or 50

CRUSTY CHICKEN BITES

½ c. real mayonnaise.. Preheat oven to 425° F. In a small bowl, mix mayon-
1 tsp. dry mustard naise, mustard, onion and pepper until well blended;
1 tsp. instant minced set aside.
   onion
¼ tsp. freshly ground
   pepper

½ c. fine dry bread .... In a pie plate or other shallow container, combine
   crumbs crumbs, sesame seeds and parsley.
¼ c. sesame seeds
2 tsp. minced fresh
   parsley

2 c. cubed............ Coat chicken with mayonnaise mixture, then crumb
   cooked chicken mixture. Place cubes on ungreased baking sheets.
Bake for 10 to 12 minutes or until lightly browned.

¾ c. real mayonnaise.. In a small bowl or cup, mix mayonnaise, honey and
1½ tbsp. honey mustard until smooth.
1½ tsp. Dijon mustard

Serve hot chicken cubes with wooden picks and
honey dip.

Makes about 40

LACE-CAPPED MUSHROOMS

"The melted cheese is what gives the lacy look."

12 to 14 med.......... Preheat oven to 375° F. Remove stems from mush-
   mushrooms rooms; brush caps with some of the butter or mar-
⅓ c. butter or garine. Place mushrooms, rounded-side down, on
   margarine, melted an ungreased baking sheet.

¼ c. cracker crumbs... In a small bowl, mix remaining butter or margarine,
¼ c. finely shredded crumbs, cheese, marjoram, garlic and pepper,
   Swiss cheese blending well. Fill each mushroom cap with 1 tea-
   (1 oz.) spoon filling, mounding slightly in center. Bake for 5
½ tsp. dried marjoram minutes or until warm, then broil 6 inches from heat
   leaves, crushed source until golden and lacy. Serve hot.
1 clove garlic, minced
⅛ tsp. freshly ground
   pepper

Makes 12 to 14

SPINACH BITES WITH LEMON MAYONNAISE

1 pkg. (10 oz.) frozen
   chopped spinach,
   thawed and well
   drained
1 c. herb-seasoned
   stuffing mix
½ c. grated Parmesan
   cheese
2 eggs, lightly beaten
⅓ c. butter or
   margarine, melted
1 tsp. instant minced
   onion
   Dash of ground
   nutmeg

Lightly grease baking sheets. In a small bowl, mix spinach, stuffing mix, cheese, eggs, butter or margarine, onion and nutmeg until well blended. Shape into balls using 1 teaspoon of the mixture for each ball; place on baking sheets. Cover and refrigerate at least 4 hours or freeze until ready to bake.

½ c. real mayonnaise
1 tbsp. fresh lemon
   juice
1 tsp. sugar
1 tsp. Dijon mustard
   Dash of hot pepper
   sauce
¼ c. dairy sour cream

Preheat oven to 350° F. Bake spinach bites for 10 to 15 minutes or until bottoms are starting to brown. In a small bowl, mix mayonnaise, lemon juice, sugar, mustard and hot pepper sauce; blend until smooth. Stir in sour cream.

To serve, spear warm spinach bites with wooden picks and dip in lemon mayonnaise.

Makes about 65

NOTES:

49

BAKED MUSHROOM ROLLS

1½ c. chopped ....
  mushrooms
  (about ¼ lb.)
½ c. finely chopped
  onion
1 tbsp. vegetable oil
1 tbsp. butter or
  margarine
	Grease a baking sheet. In a medium skillet over medium-high heat, sauté mushrooms and onion in oil and butter or margarine for 3 minutes or until golden.

1 tbsp. all-purpose ....
  flour
¼ tsp. dried thyme
  leaves, crushed
¼ tsp. salt
⅛ tsp. freshly ground
  pepper
3 tbsp. milk
	Stir in flour, thyme, salt and pepper. Cook and stir over medium heat for 1 to 2 minutes. Add milk. Stirring, bring to a boil and boil until thickened. Remove from heat.

10 slices white bread ...	Place bread on a clean dry surface; trim crusts. With a rolling pin, roll bread until very thin.
3 tbsp. butter or ...... margarine, melted	Brush bread with butter or margarine and spread each slice with 1 tablespoon of the mushroom mixture. Roll up from the narrow end and place seam-side down on the baking sheet. Cover and freeze for 1 hour or chill at least 2 hours before baking.

Preheat oven to 425° F. Bake for 8 to 10 minutes or until golden brown. Serve on a warming tray.

Makes 20

CLEANING MUSHROOMS

The question of how to clean and store mushrooms is often raised. Lovely white mushrooms with little grit are no problem. When there is a considerable amount of dirt on the surface, it is imperative to remove it thoroughly. It is never advisable to soak mushrooms. If necessary, simply rinse briefly and wipe with a damp cloth or paper towel. Any bruising will show up as a dark blemish, so handle raw mushrooms gently if appearance is important. Store unwashed fresh mushrooms in a large uncovered container in the refrigerator. Air circulation is important. If purchased fresh, mushrooms will keep for several days before cooking.

FRIED CHEESE CUBES

1½ c. fine soft bread .... crumbs ¾ c. wheat germ ¼ tsp. ground red pepper	Lightly grease a baking sheet. In a medium bowl, mix crumbs, wheat germ and pepper.
3 eggs	In a small bowl, beat eggs well.
8 oz. Fontina, Havarti, Monterey Jack, Edam, Cheddar, Muenster or Swiss cheese, cut in ½″ cubes	Dip cheese cubes into eggs, then into crumb mixture, coating well; dip and coat again. Place on baking sheet and freeze for 30 minutes or cover and chill at least 1 hour.
Vegetable oil	Pour vegetable oil into a large skillet to a depth of 1 inch. Heat oil over medium-high heat to 375° F. Place cheese cubes, a few at a time, in the oil and fry for 30 to 60 seconds or until a deep golden brown. Remove with a slotted spoon and drain on paper towels. Keep warm until all cheese is fried. Serve immediately on a warming tray with wooden picks.

Makes 50 to 60

ITALIAN CHEESE PUFFS

½ c. real mayonnaise.. ½ c. grated Parmesan cheese ¼ c. minced onion 1 tbsp. minced fresh parsley 1 tsp. Italian herb seasoning, crushed	Preheat oven to 375° F. In a small bowl, mix mayonnaise, cheese, onion, parsley and Italian herb seasoning until blended.
4 slices sandwich ..... bread Paprika	Cut crusts from bread. Spread each slice with ¼ cup of the cheese mixture. Cut into four triangles and place on a baking sheet. Sprinkle with paprika. Bake for 10 to 12 minutes or until bubbly and golden. Serve on a warming tray.

Makes 16

TOMATO QUICHE

"The tomatoes form a nice, colorful layer. Don't use a commercial pie shell. You need a 10-inch shell to hold all the filling."

1 c. chopped onion ...
2 tbsp. butter or margarine
3 lg. tomatoes, peeled, seeded, chopped and drained
1 tsp. salt
¼ tsp. freshly ground pepper
¼ tsp. dried thyme leaves, crushed

Preheat oven to 425° F. In a large skillet over medium-high heat, sauté onion in butter or margarine until limp. Add tomatoes, salt, pepper and thyme. Cook over high heat for 8 to 12 minutes or until liquid is almost evaporated.

2 c. shredded.........
Monterey Jack cheese (8 oz.)
1 baked 10" pie shell

Place 1 cup of the cheese in pie shell. Spoon on tomato mixture and top with remaining cheese.

4 eggs ....
1½ c. half-and-half or whipping cream
Chopped green onions

In a small mixer bowl at high speed, beat eggs until foamy; at low speed beat in half-and-half or cream. Pour over mixture in pie shell. Bake in lower one-third of the oven for 10 minutes; reduce heat to 325° F. and bake 45 minutes longer or until a knife inserted near center comes out clean. Garnish with green onions.

Let stand for 10 minutes before cutting into wedges.

Makes 12 servings

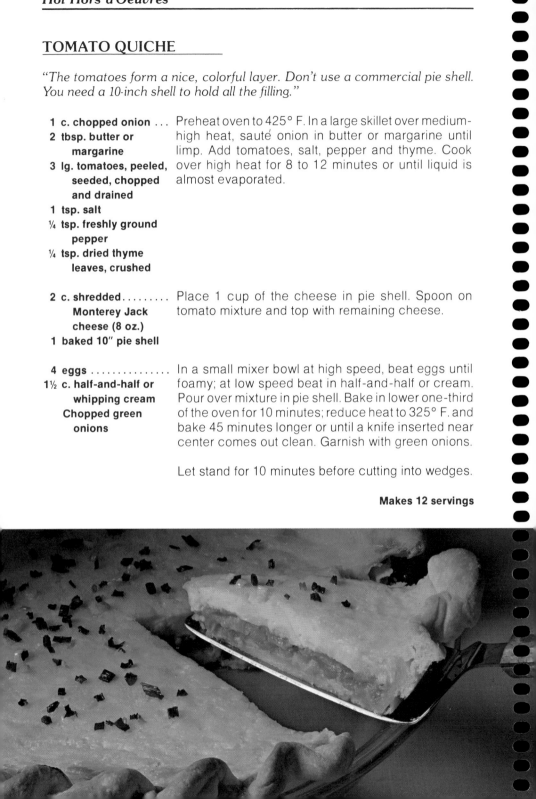

GREEK CHEESE TRIANGLES

"Set aside a few hours to stock up your freezer with these special tidbits. Take out what you need and heat in a 350° F. oven."

1 pkg. (8 oz.) cream cheese, softened ... In a small mixer bowl at medium speed, beat cheeses, parsley, dill and garlic powder for 3 minutes or until smooth and creamy.

¼ lb. feta cheese

1 tbsp. minced fresh parsley

1 tsp. dried dill weed, crushed

½ tsp. garlic powder

1 lb. phyllo dough leaves, about 16″ x 12″ each ..... Preheat oven to 350° F. Grease baking sheets. Unfold dough and cover with a damp towel. Place two phyllo leaves on a clean surface and brush with butter. Cut into six strips, 16 x 2-inches each. Place 1 teaspoon cheese mixture at the end of one strip. Fold one corner over to opposite side to make a triangle. Continue to fold to end of strip (like folding a flag). Fill and fold remaining strips. Repeat until all phyllo leaves have been used. Place triangles on baking sheets, leaving ½-inch space between triangles. Bake for 18 to 20 minutes or until golden brown.* Serve hot.

¾ c. real butter, melted

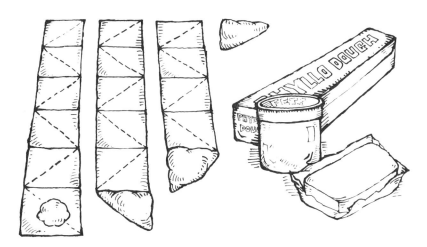

*These appetizers can be made and baked ahead; cover and refrigerate overnight or freeze. To serve, place triangles on ungreased baking sheets and bake in a preheated 350° F. oven for 10 to 15 minutes or until heated through.

Makes about 80

PITA PIZZAS

¼ **lb. bulk pork** .... **sausage, crumbled**	Preheat oven to 425° F. In a 10-inch skillet over medium-high heat, cook sausage until lightly browned and no longer pink. Remove with a slotted spoon to a small bowl; set aside. Drain all but 1 tablespoon of the fat from skillet.
2 **tbsp. chopped** ...... **onion** ½ **c. sliced fresh mushrooms** ½ **tsp. Italian herb seasoning** **Dash of garlic powder**	Sauté onion for 2 minutes or until golden. Add mushrooms and sauté for 1 minute. Stir in sausage, herb seasoning and garlic powder, mixing well; remove from heat.
4 **pita bread rounds,** .. **6″ each** 3 **tbsp. olive oil** ½ **c. tomato sauce** ¾ **to 1 c. shredded mozzarella cheese**	Place pita rounds on a baking sheet. Brush top of each round with oil. Spread 2 tablespoons tomato sauce on each round. Sprinkle one-fourth of the sausage mixture on top of each round; top with one-fourth of the cheese. Bake for 5 minutes or until cheese is bubbly. Cut each round into six wedges and arrange on a warm serving plate or warming tray. Serve hot.

Makes 24

BACON-CHEESE ROLLS

10 **slices sandwich** ..... **bread** 2 **tbsp. prepared mustard (optional)** 10 **slices bacon** 4 **oz. Cheddar cheese, cut in sticks**	Preheat oven to 475° F. Trim crusts from bread; cut each slice in half lengthwise. Flatten slightly with a rolling pin. Spread with optional mustard. Cut each bacon strip in half crosswise. Place bread halves on bacon halves, matching ends. Place cheese sticks crosswise at one end. Roll up and fasten with a wooden pick. Place seam-side down on a wire rack set in a 15½ x 10½ x 1-inch jelly roll pan.* Bake for 8 to 10 minutes or until bacon is crisped.

Serve hot on a warming tray with wooden picks.

*Rolls can be prepared to this step. Cover and refrigerate. Increase baking time to 12 to 15 minutes.

Makes 20

SALMON BALLS WITH DILL SAUCE

1 c. dairy sour cream . . . In a small bowl, mix sour cream and dill. Spoon into a
1 tsp. dried dill weed,   serving bowl; cover and chill.
    crushed

1 can (15½ oz.) . . . . Preheat oven to 350° F. Lightly grease two baking
    salmon   sheets. Drain, bone and flake salmon. In a medium bowl,
1 c. fresh bread crumbs mix salmon, bread crumbs, eggs, celery, onion,
2 eggs, lightly beaten   parsley, lemon juice and salt until well blended.
⅓ c. minced celery
2 tbsp. minced onion
2 tbsp. chopped fresh
    parsley
1 tbsp. fresh lemon
    juice
⅛ tsp. salt

⅔ c. crushed . . . . Form a level tablespoon of mixture into a ball, roll
    corn flakes   in corn flakes and place on a baking sheet. Repeat
                           with remaining mixture. Bake for 10 minutes or
                           until set and hot.

3 lemons, cut in . . . . . . To serve, arrange salmon balls on a warming tray.
    small wedges   Serve with dill sauce and lemon. Provide small plates
                           and tongs or a pickle fork.

Makes 36 balls

PLANNING A COCKTAIL BUFFET

The cocktail buffet is a very flexible and convenient way to entertain a fairly large number of people, and the guests seem to like the informality of walking around and visiting while enjoying their food. For the first hour or so, plan hors d'oeuvres that can be passed around on trays or set on tables around the room. Set up the beverage area out of the flow of traffic to avoid congestion. If you don't have help, assign the drink preparation to the man of the house or a good friend while you attend to the food. Place the buffet table away from the wall so people can walk around all sides; keep it close to the kitchen if possible. Choose foods that are substantial, but easy to eat. Small sandwiches and meatballs are good items to build a menu around, for example Mexican Meatballs (see page 41), Pork Spring Rolls with Sweet and Sour Sauce (see page 46), Marinated Pork Tenderloin (see page 56) or Water Chestnut Meatballs (see page 42). Make use of the chafing dish and other warming devices to keep hot foods hot. Dessert is optional. Homemade cookies are always welcome; place them near the coffee or pass them yourself as you visit.

MARINATED PORK TENDERLOIN

½ c. soy sauce .... In a shallow 1½-quart glass baking dish, mix soy
¼ c. firmly packed   sauce, brown sugar, oil, ginger, mustard and garlic.
   brown sugar
2 tbsp. vegetable oil
1 tsp. ground ginger
½ tsp. dry mustard
2 cloves garlic, minced

1¼ lb. pork tenderloin.. Place meat in dish and turn to coat surface. Cover
and refrigerate for 12 hours or overnight, turning
several times. Drain, reserving ¼ cup of the marinade.

Preheat oven to 325° F. Place meat on rack in a shallow roasting pan. Bake for 1 hour and 15 minutes or
until meat thermometer reaches 170° F. Cool, wrap
and chill.

¾ c. water .... About 30 minutes before serving, slice meat thinly.
24 sm. dinner or   Place in a chafing dish. In a small bowl, mix water and
   Parkerhouse rolls,   ¼ cup reserved marinade. Pour over meat. Serve hot
   warmed   with rolls.

Makes about 24 sandwiches

MOLASSES BARBECUE FRANKFURTERS

2 c. tomato sauce ..... In a medium saucepan, mix tomato sauce, molasses,
½ c. molasses   vinegar, oil, onion, Worcestershire sauce, mustard,
½ c. vinegar   orange rind and salt until blended. Over medium heat,
2 tbsp. vegetable oil bring to a boil; reduce heat to low and simmer,
4 tsp. instant minced uncovered, stirring occasionally, for 20 to 25 minutes
   onion   or until mixture is thickened.
4 tsp. Worcestershire
   sauce
1 tbsp. dry mustard
1 tsp. grated orange
   rind
½ tsp. salt

1 pkg. (16 oz.) frank-.. Add frankfurters to sauce and heat through.
   furters, cut in
   1" pieces

Transfer to a chafing dish and serve with wooden
picks.

Makes about 12 servings

chapter 4 CONTENTS

Pictured on the preceding page are Watercress Sandwiches, Herbed Radish Canapés and Open-Faced Buffet Sandwiches.

Cold Hors d'Oeuvres

WATERCRESS SANDWICHES

"Watercress may be hard to find, but when you can, make these unique little triangles."

1 jar (4 oz.) whole pimientos, well drained	With small aspic cutters or tiny cookie cutters, cut decorative designs from the pimientos; set aside.
2 oz. cream cheese, softened 4 tsp. real mayonnaise Few drops of fresh lemon juice ¼ c. minced water-cress (about 2 bunches) Salt and freshly ground pepper	In a small bowl, mix cream cheese, mayonnaise and lemon juice. Stir in watercress and salt and pepper to taste until well blended.
6 slices sandwich bread	Trim crusts from bread. Spread each slice with 1 tablespoon watercress mixture. Cut in triangles and garnish with pimiento cut-outs.

Makes 24

NOTES:

BOMBAY CELERY STICKS

"A nice crunchy-sweet filling makes these different."

2 oz. cream cheese, ... In a small bowl, mix cream cheese, peanuts and
    softened   chutney until well blended.
3 tbsp. chopped salted
    peanuts
1 tbsp. chopped
    chutney

8 ribs (8" ea.)......... Stuff each celery rib with 1 tablespoon cheese
    celery   mixture. Cover and chill.

To serve, cut in 2-inch pieces.

Makes 32 pieces

SHRIMP-STUFFED ARTICHOKE HEARTS

1 pkg. (9 oz.) frozen.. Cook artichokes according to package directions,
    artichoke hearts   adding lemon juice, garlic and salt to the water. Drain
2 tsp. fresh lemon   well on paper towels until cool.
    juice
1 clove garlic, crushed
¼ tsp. salt

1 pkg. (6 oz.) frozen.. In a small bowl, mix shrimp, bread crumbs, may-
    sm. shrimp,   onnaise, celery, parsley, lemon juice, chives, Wor-
    thawed and   cestershire sauce and salt and pepper to taste
    chopped   until blended. Fill each artichoke half with 1 tea-
3 tbsp. soft bread   spoon of the shrimp mixture. Garnish each with an
    crumbs   olive slice. Cover and chill for 30 minutes.
2 tbsp. real
    mayonnaise
2 tbsp. minced celery
1 tbsp. minced fresh
    parsley
1 tsp. fresh lemon
    juice
1 tsp. chopped chives
¼ tsp. Worcestershire
    sauce
  Salt and freshly
    ground pepper
  Ripe olive slices

Makes about 18

CURRIED TURKEY CANAPÉS

1½ c. finely chopped ... cooked turkey ½ c. minced celery 1 hard-cooked egg, chopped 1 jar (2 oz.) chopped pimiento, drained 1 tbsp. minced onion 1 clove garlic, minced ½ tsp. fresh lemon juice ½ tsp. curry powder ½ tsp. salt Pinch of dry mustard	In a medium bowl, mix turkey, celery, egg, pimiento, onion, garlic, lemon juice, curry powder, salt and mustard until well blended.
¾ c. real .... mayonnaise	Stir in mayonnaise until moistened. Cover and chill.
Crackers .... Cracker Sealer (see page 67) Fresh parsley sprigs or sliced olives	Seal crackers with Cracker Sealer. Spread about 1 tablespoon of the turkey mixture on each cracker and garnish with parsley or olives.

Makes about 24

SALAMI-CONE CANAPÉS

4 oz. cream cheese, ... softened 4 to 5 tsp. apricot or pineapple preserves	In a small bowl, mix cream cheese and preserves. Fill a star-tipped pastry bag with cream cheese mixture; set aside.
1 jar (5 oz.) pine- ..... apple-flavored processed cheese spread 9 slices sandwich bread	In a double boiler, melt the cheese spread. Cheese will be a soft consistency and easily spreadable. Trim crust from bread; spread each slice with 1 tablespoon spread. Cut in triangles.
18 slices (3″ diameter... ea.) salami 36 sm. pimiento- stuffed or pitted ripe olives	Cut the salami slices in half and roll each half into a cone. With a wooden pick, skewer an olive, then the salami cone. Fasten the salami cones to the bread triangles. Pipe cream cheese mixture into each cone. Cover and chill.

Makes 36

HERBED RADISH CANAPÉS

2 tbsp. real butter..... In a small bowl, mix butter, radishes, chives, dill
2 tsp. minced red   and salt and pepper to taste until well blended.
   radishes
1 tsp. chopped chives
⅛ tsp. dried dill weed,
   crushed
   Salt and freshly
   ground pepper

3 slices sandwich..... Trim crust from bread. Spread each slice with
   bread   1 tablespoon butter mixture. Cut in triangles and
6 to 7 red radishes,   top each with three radish slices. Cover and chill.
   very thinly sliced

   Fresh parsley....... To serve, garnish each with a parsley sprig if desired.
   sprigs (optional)

Makes 12

VEGETABLES A LA GRECQUE

"A fantastic looking tray for a cocktail buffet."

2 c. olive oil or .... In a medium saucepan over medium heat, bring
   vegetable oil or   oil, celery, garlic, lemon juice, vinegar, hot pepper
   a combination   sauce, salt, coriander, rosemary, thyme, sage,
1 lg. rib celery, cut   bay leaf and fennel seeds to a boil; reduce heat
   in ½" slices   to low and simmer for 5 minutes. Remove from
3 cloves garlic, minced heat; set aside.
⅓ c. fresh lemon
   juice
2 tbsp. cider vinegar
6 drops hot pepper
   sauce
2 tsp. salt
1½ tsp. ground
   coriander
1½ tsp. dried rosemary
   leaves, crushed
1½ tsp. dried thyme
   leaves, crushed
1½ tsp. dried sage
   leaves, crushed
1 lg. bay leaf
¼ to ½ tsp. fennel
   seeds, crushed

continued on next page . . .

Vegetables a la Grecque continued...

4 c. water .... In a 2-quart saucepan, mix water and bouillon.
1 tbsp. chicken Bring to a boil over high heat and keep boiling.
bouillon granules

2 c. ¼" sliced .... Place carrots in a wire basket and plunge into the
carrots boiling bouillon; return to a boil. Reduce heat to
2 c. broccoli flowerets, low and simmer for 4 minutes or until crisp-tender.
cut in bite-size Lift out basket and rinse carrots under cold
pieces running water; drain. Place carrots in a small bowl.
2 c. cauliflower Repeat process with broccoli and cauliflower,
flowerets, cut in cooking only 2 minutes or until crisp-tender; place
bite-size pieces vegetables in separate bowls. Place zucchini
2 c. unpeeled ¼" and mushrooms in separate bowls. Pour about ½
sliced zucchini cup marinade over each vegetable and stir to
16 med. fresh mush- coat well. Cover and refrigerate for 12 hours or
rooms, cut in half overnight, stirring several times.

About 4 hours before serving, remove vegetables
from refrigerator and allow to come to room temperature.

Whole fresh .... To serve, drain each vegetable well. Place an at-
pineapple, tractive clean whole pineapple, eggplant or arti-
eggplant or choke in the center of a large tray. Arrange indivi-
artichoke dual vegetables in spoke fashion on the tray. Cut
5 lemons, sliced lemon slices in half crosswise and place a row of
slices, cut-side down, between each group of veg-
etables. Place wooden picks in a small container
beside the tray.

Serves 20 to 24

GRAVAD LAX (Marinated Salmon)

"I don't make this often, but it is always enjoyed when I do. You need to allow a few days to get it ready."

2 tbsp. salt . . . . In a small bowl, mix salt, sugar, pepper, dill weed
2 tbsp. sugar and seeds. Sprinkle about 2 tablespoons of the
1 tbsp. cracked mixture over the bottom of a shallow glass baking
   pepper dish.
1½ tsp. dried dill
   weed, crushed
¾ tsp. dill seeds

1 salmon fillet with . . . . Place salmon, skin-side down, in the dish. Sprinkle
   skin (1 lb.), with remaining salt mixture. Cover with plastic
   boned wrap and place a weight on the fish. Refrigerate
for 48 hours, spooning the marinade over the
fish each morning and night.

To serve, remove salmon from marinade, scrape away marinade and pat fish dry with paper towels. Place skin-side down on a cutting board. With a sharp knife, shave the salmon.

Melba toast rounds . . Serve on toast rounds or crackers with mustard
   or crackers sauce.
Mustard Sauce
   (see below)

Makes 16 (1-ounce) servings

MUSTARD SAUCE FOR GRAVAD LAX

⅓ c. vegetable oil . . . . . In a small bowl, mix oil, mustard, sugar, sour
2 tbsp. Dijon mustard cream, wine, salt and dill weed until well blended.
1 tbsp. sugar
2 tsp. dairy sour
   cream
2 tsp. dry white wine
¼ tsp. salt
¼ tsp. dried dill
   weed, crushed

Serve with Gravad Lax or with cold cuts.

Makes about ⅔ cup

NOTES:

Making Fancy Garnishes

TOMATO ROSES

For a pretty and colorful rosette, start with a medium, firm tomato. With a sharp paring knife, cut a circle at the base but do not cut all the way through. Continue peeling off a thin circular strip round and round the tomato. Use a sawing motion and don't worry if the strip is not perfectly even; it will look more natural if it is irregular. Curl the strip so it sits nicely on its base. If you have a smaller strip left, curl it tightly and place it in the middle.

CARROT CURLS, ACCORDIONS AND FLOWERS

With a vegetable peeler, slice thin, wide strips from a carrot. Roll up each slice and fasten with a wooden pick. Or, thread each slice in a zigzag fashion onto a wooden pick. Or, fold three or four slices in half and alternately thread onto a wooden pick, like petals, and secure center with a round slice of carrot threaded in the center. Place curls, accordions and flowers in a bowl and cover with ice water until crisped. Drain well before serving and remove wooden picks from curls and accordions.

GREEN ONION OR CELERY BRUSHES

With a sharp paring knife, trim ends from green onions or celery ribs. At one or both ends, make lengthwise slashes about 2″ long. Rotate and slash again, creating a brush effect. Place in a bowl and cover with ice water until crisped and ends have curled. Drain well before serving.

SWEET PICKLE FANS

With a sharp paring knife, make several lengthwise slices from one end of the pickle almost to the opposite end; spread slices apart to form a fan. Small pickles have a more dainty appearance.

RADISH ROSES

With a sharp paring knife, cut off root tip and green tops. Make four or five thin slices around the radish, cutting from top towards bottom, being careful not to slice through. Place in a bowl and cover with ice water until petals open. Drain well before serving.

SCORED CUCUMBERS

Select a thin cucumber. Run the tines of a fork lengthwise down through the cucumber peel. Repeat scoring around the cucumber. With a sharp paring knife, slice crosswise or on the diagonal.

FROSTED SANDWICH LOAF

12 slices firm sand- .... Arrange three slices of bread, side by side, on a
wich bread, serving plate, edges touching. Spread with Ham
crusts removed Filling, top with three bread slices. Spread with
Ham Filling (see Chicken Filling, top with three more bread slices.
below) Spread with Egg Filling, top with three bread slices.
Chicken Filling Press layers together gently. Wrap loaf securely
(see page 67) in foil or plastic wrap. Refrigerate several hours.
Egg Filling
(see page 67)

2 pkg. (8 oz. ea.) ...... About 1 hour before serving, in a small mixer bowl
cream cheese, at low speed, beat cream cheese and milk until
softened smooth and of spreading consistency. Reserve
2 to 3 tbsp. milk 1 cup. Unwrap loaf. Spread sides and top of loaf with
cream cheese mixture.

Whole pimiento, ... Decorate loaf with pimiento, green onion tops
cut in decorative and almonds or as desired. Pipe remaining cheese
shapes mixture in a border around base and top edges
Green onion tops of loaf. Slice to serve.
Toasted slivered or
sliced almonds

Makes 15 (¾-inch) servings

HAM FILLING

1 can (6¾ oz.) .... In a small bowl, mix ham, mayonnaise, relish, horse-
chunk ham, radish and mustard until well blended. Cover and
drained and flaked chill.
¼ c. real mayonnaise
2 tbsp. sweet pickle
relish
1 tsp. prepared
horseradish
¼ tsp. dry mustard

Makes about 1 cup

CHICKEN FILLING

1 cooked whole ...... In a small bowl, mix chicken, mayonnaise, celery,
   chicken breast,   almonds, parsley, lemon juice and pepper to taste
   minced*   until well blended. Cover and chill.
6 to 8 tbsp. real
   mayonnaise
2 tbsp. minced celery
2 tbsp. chopped
   toasted almonds
2 tbsp. minced fresh
   parsley
½ tsp. fresh lemon
   juice
   Freshly ground
   pepper

*Or use two 5-ounce cans chunk white chicken, drained and minced.

Makes about 1⅓ cups

EGG FILLING

4 hard-cooked .... In a small bowl, mix eggs, mayonnaise, onion,
   eggs, minced   salt, dill weed and mustard until well blended. Cover
¼ c. real mayonnaise   and chill.
1 tsp. minced onion
¼ tsp. salt
⅛ tsp. dried dill weed,
   crushed
   Pinch of dry mustard

Makes about 1 cup

CRACKER SEALER

"This is a clever way to keep bread and crackers from becoming soggy."

¼ tsp. unflavored...... In a small saucepan, mix gelatin and water; let
   gelatin   stand for 1 minute. Stir over medium heat until
1 tbsp. water   gelatin is dissolved. Remove from heat. Stir in
½ c. real mayonnaise   mayonnaise. Spread thinly on crackers, toast rounds,
   bread, etc. Top as desired to make canapés. Cover
   and chill up to 3 hours.

Makes ½ cup

67

PETITS CHOUX (Tiny Cream Puffs)

4 eggs . . . . Preheat oven to 400°F. Break eggs into a small bowl; set aside.

1 c. water . . . . In a medium saucepan over medium heat, bring
½ c. butter or water and butter or margarine to a rolling boil; re-
margarine duce heat to low. Add flour all at once and stir vig-
1 c. all-purpose flour orously with a wire whisk or wooden spoon for 1 minute or until the mixture forms a ball. Remove from heat. Add eggs all at once and continue beating until mixture is smooth. Drop dough, 1 teaspoonful at a time, about 1½ inches apart, onto ungreased baking sheets. Bake for 22 to 25 minutes or until golden brown. Remove from baking sheets; cool on wire racks away from drafts.*

Chicken Filling . . . . . To serve, cut tops from Petits Choux; fill with de-
(see page 67), sired filling.
Ham Filling
(see page 66),
or filling of
your choice

*Petits Choux can be frozen. To re-crisp, place in preheated 350°F. oven for 5 to 10 minutes; cool.

Makes about 5 dozen (1¼-inch each)

CHEESE PETITS CHOUX

Make Petits Choux with the following changes: Beat 1 cup shredded Swiss cheese and ½ teaspoon dry mustard into mixture after eggs have been beaten in.

STORING FANCY SANDWICHES

Dainty, decorative sandwiches are always popular at an afternoon gathering or for a cocktail buffet. They can be made ahead in a variety of shapes and flavors, and keep well until serving time if stored properly. Line the bottom of a shallow container with a damp tea towel; cover the towel with waxed paper. Arrange a few layers of sandwiches with waxed paper between the layers. Cover tightly with foil and refrigerate until serving time. Certain sandwiches freeze well, but do not freeze those made with mayonnaise, sour cream, lettuce, tomato or hard-cooked egg whites.

CUCUMBER SANDWICHES

2 oz. cream cheese,... softened
1 tbsp. minced onion
1 tsp. real mayonnaise
Salt and freshly ground pepper

In a small bowl, mix cream cheese, onion, mayonnaise and salt and pepper to taste until well blended; set aside.

5 slices white .... sandwich bread
5 slices whole wheat bread
¼ c. real butter
1 cucumber (2″ diameter) peeled and sliced ⅛″ thick

With a 2-inch round cookie or biscuit cutter, cut two rounds from each slice of bread. Lightly butter the white rounds. Spread whole wheat rounds with cream cheese mixture; top each with a slice of cucumber. Cover with a white round. Cover and chill.

To serve, cut in half and arrange sandwiches on a platter, half with white rounds on top and half with whole wheat on top.

Makes 20

PITA WEDGES WITH TUNA FILLING

3 tbsp. real .... mayonnaise
¼ tsp. fresh lemon juice
1 drop hot pepper sauce
1 can (6½ oz.) tuna, drained and flaked
8 slices bacon, fried and crumbled
¼ c. minced celery
1 tbsp. minced onion
Salt and freshly ground pepper

In a medium bowl, mix mayonnaise, lemon juice and hot pepper sauce. Stir in tuna, bacon, celery, onion and salt and pepper to taste.

3 pita bread .... rounds, 6″ each
24 sm. pimiento-stuffed olives

Cut pita rounds in half. Fill each pocket with about 2 heaping tablespoons of the filling; cut in quarters. Fasten each with an olive on a wooden pick.

Makes 24 servings

OPEN-FACED BUFFET SANDWICHES

"Pickled beet slices, crumbled bacon and sour cream are nice additions, but add them just before serving."

Sourdough rye, ... pumpernickel or firm white bread	Trim crusts from bread if desired. Cut into desired shapes. Spread entire surface of each slice to the very edge with butter, margarine or mayonnaise.
Softened butter or margarine or real mayonnaise Lettuce leaves	Place a lettuce leaf on each slice.
Cold rare roast ..... beef, thinly sliced	Top with one or more of the desired sandwich toppings. Season with salt and pepper to taste.
Cold roast pork, thinly sliced	
Thinly sliced ham	
Thinly sliced salami	
Pickled herring, drained	
Whole lg. shrimp, cooked, shelled and deveined	
Sardines	
Anchovy fillets, drained	
Thinly sliced smoked salmon	
Sliced cheese	
Hard-cooked egg slices	
Salt and freshly ground pepper	
Thinly sliced .... tomato	Decoratively top with one of the garnishes listed to complement the sandwich. Arrange prepared
Cucumber slices	sandwiches on a large platter. Cover and refrig-
Raw onion rings	erate several hours.
Pickle fans	
Caviar	
Fresh parsley, dill or watercress sprigs	

Makes as many as you wish

NOTES:

SHRIMP SMØRBRØD

6 oz. cooked tiny ..... In a medium bowl, mix
shrimp shrimp, peas, mayon-
¼ c. canned tiny naise, lemon juice and
peas, drained salt just to blend.
2 tbsp. real
mayonnaise
Few drops of fresh
lemon juice
Pinch of salt

3 slices firm sour- ..... Trim crusts from bread
dough rye bread, if desired. Spread each
cut in half slice of bread with butter
¼ c. real butter, and top with a lettuce
softened leaf. Mound about ¼ cup
Lettuce leaves shrimp mixture on top of
lettuce. Cover and refrig-
erate several hours.

Very thinly .... To serve, cut lemon slices from edge to center;
sliced lemon twist and place on shrimp mixture.

Makes 6 servings

RED CAVIAR AND CREAM CHEESE ROUNDS

"An elegant and dainty treat for caviar lovers."

1 pkg. (3 oz.) cream ... In a small bowl, mix cream cheese, lemon juice
cheese, softened and salt and white pepper to taste.
Few drops of fresh
lemon juice
Salt and white
pepper

27 to 30 Melba .... Spread each toast round or cracker with about
rounds or ½ teaspoon cream cheese mixture. Top with about
crackers ¼ teaspoon caviar, a slice of lemon and a sprig
1 jar (2 oz.) red of parsley.
caviar, drained
Very thinly sliced
lemons
Fresh parsley sprigs

Makes 27 to 30

NOTES:

FANCY DEVILED EGGS

8 hard-cooked .... eggs, cut in half lengthwise	Remove yolks from eggs and place in a medium bowl; cover whites and chill. Mash yolks.
½ c. real .... mayonnaise 1 tbsp. Dijon mustard 1 tbsp. minced onion 2 to 3 tsp. capers, drained (optional) ¾ tsp. dried dill weed, crushed ½ tsp. grated lemon rind ⅛ tsp. freshly ground pepper	Add mayonnaise, mustard, onion, optional capers, dill weed, lemon rind and pepper; stir until well blended.
1 pkg. (6 oz.) .... frozen crab meat, thawed, drained and flaked	Stir in crab meat; cover and chill at least 2 hours.
Pimiento strips ..... Fresh parsley sprigs	Just before serving, fill egg white halves with crab mixture. Garnish with pimiento and parsley.

Makes 16 halves

CRAB-STUFFED CHERRY TOMATOES

1 pkg. (6 oz.) frozen .. crab meat, thawed and flaked 1 pt. cherry tomatoes	Drain crab meat on several layers of paper towels. Thinly slice tops and bottoms from tomatoes. With a small melon ball cutter, remove pulp and drain upside-down on paper towels.
¼ c. real .... mayonnaise 1 tbsp. minced fresh parsley ½ tsp. dry mustard Pinch of salt	In a small bowl, mix crab meat, mayonnaise, parsley, mustard and salt until well blended; stuff tomatoes. Chill at least 30 minutes.
Fresh parsley or .... watercress sprigs	Serve on a tray garnished with parsley or watercress.

Makes about 24

chapter 5 CONTENTS

Pictured on the preceding page are Savory Popcorn, Sugar 'N' Spice Nuts, Bridge Nibbles and Chow Mein Snack.

SAVORY POPCORN

2 qt. (8 c.) . . . .
    popped corn
¼ c. butter or mar-
    garine, melted
3 tbsp. grated
    American cheese
    food*
½ tsp. onion powder
¼ tsp. hickory-smoked
    salt

In a large bowl, place popped corn. Drizzle with butter or margarine. Sprinkle with cheese, onion powder and hickory-smoked salt. Toss lightly until corn is evenly coated. Store in an airtight container in a cool place.

*Grated Parmesan cheese may be substituted for American cheese food.

Makes 2 quarts

SUGAR 'N' SPICE NUTS

"My favorite recipe for nuts. I make these for gifts every Christmas."

3 c. mixed unsalted . .
    nuts

Preheat oven to 275° F. Grease a 15½ x 10½ x 1-inch jelly roll pan. Place nuts in a large bowl; set aside.

1 egg white . . . .
1 tbsp. orange juice
    or water
⅔ c. sugar
1 tbsp. grated orange
    rind (optional)
1 tsp. ground
    cinnamon
½ tsp. ground ginger
½ tsp. ground allspice
¼ tsp. salt

In a small bowl, beat egg white and orange juice or water with a fork until frothy. Add sugar, optional orange rind, spices and salt until well blended. Pour over nuts, stirring to coat well. Spread nuts on jelly roll pan, edges not touching. Bake, stirring every 15 minutes, for 45 to 55 minutes or until light brown and crisp. Cool. Store in an airtight container in a cool place.

Makes about 5 cups

MEXICAN NUTS AND SEEDS

"South-of-the-border seasonings. Serve these with chilled sangria or beer."

1½ c. salted peanuts	In a medium skillet over
½ c. salted sunflower	medium heat, stir pea-
kernels, pumpkin	nuts, kernels or seeds,
seeds or a	oil, chili, onion and garlic
combination	powders together for 5
2 tsp. vegetable oil	to 7 minutes or until
1½ tsp. chili powder	peanuts are lightly toast-
1½ tsp. onion powder	ed and spices adhere
½ tsp. garlic powder	to peanuts. Serve warm.
¼ tsp. ground cumin	

Makes 2 cups

CURRIED PECANS

"Choose mild, not hot, curry for these nut treats."

2 tbsp. vegetable oil ..	In a heavy 10-inch skillet over medium heat, stir
½ tsp. salt	together oil, salt and garlic powder.
¼ tsp. garlic powder	
2 c. pecan halves	Add pecans. Cook and stir constantly for 8 to 10 minutes or until toasted. Remove from heat.
½ tsp. curry powder ...	Sprinkle curry over pecans and stir to mix well. Serve hot or at room temperature. Store in an airtight container in a cool place.

Makes 2 cups

TACO CORN

¼ c. butter or	In a small saucepan over low heat, melt butter or
margarine	margarine. Add taco seasoning and parsley; mix
2 tbsp. taco	well.
seasoning mix	
1 tbsp. dried parsley	
flakes	
2 qt. (8 c.) popped ...	In a large bowl, place popped corn and tortilla chips.
corn	Drizzle with taco butter and toss lightly until corn is
2 c. tortilla chips,	well coated. Cool. Store in an airtight container in a
slightly broken	cool place.

Makes about 2 quarts

POPPING CORN

Today you can buy all types of corn poppers. If you have one, simply follow the directions included with your popper. Perfectly good popcorn can also be made in a large, heavy saucepan or skillet with a lid. In a 3-quart pan, use 3 tablespoons oil and ⅓ cup popcorn; in a 4-quart pan, use ¼ cup oil and ½ cup popcorn. Place the pan with the oil over medium-high heat, adding one kernel of corn. When the kernel pops, the oil is hot enough. Add the measured amount of popcorn and stir or shake the pan. Cover the pan, leaving the lid slightly ajar. When the corn starts popping, shake the pan from time to time so the unpopped corn will fall to the bottom. Continue cooking until you hear the last few pops. Remove the pan from the heat and let it stand for a minute or two. The popcorn is now ready to toss with melted butter or to use in a recipe. One-third cup of raw popcorn will make one to three quarts, depending on the brand you use.

HERBED TOAST FINGERS

"Like garlic bread with added flavor. Nice and crisp."

½ c. real butter, softened .... In a small bowl, mix butter, olives, green onion, parsley, basil, thyme, tarragon and marjoram; blend well. Cover and let stand for 30 minutes to develop flavor.

1 tbsp. minced ripe olives

1 tbsp. minced green onion

1 tbsp. minced fresh parsley

½ tsp. dried basil leaves, crushed

¼ tsp. dried thyme leaves, crushed

¼ tsp. dried tarragon leaves, crushed

¼ tsp. dried marjoram leaves, crushed

12 slices white bread ... Preheat oven to 250°F. On a cutting board, trim crusts from bread and spread each slice with about 1½ teaspoons of the herb butter. Cut each slice into three strips. Place on ungreased baking sheets and bake for 25 to 35 minutes or until crisp and golden. Cool on wire racks. Store in an airtight container in a cool place.

Makes 36

SMOKY ALMONDS

2 c. whole almonds ...	Preheat oven to 350°F.
2 tsp. butter or margarine	In a jelly roll pan, spread nuts and dot with butter or margarine. Bake for 1 minute or until butter or margarine is melted. Stir nuts to coat. Bake 10 minutes longer or until golden.
3 tbsp. grated .... **Parmesan cheese**	Sprinkle nuts with cheese, hickory-smoked salt and
1 tsp. hickory-smoked salt	red pepper. Stir to coat well. Bake 3 minutes
Dash of ground red pepper	longer. Cool on a wire rack. Store in an airtight container in a cool place.

Makes 2 cups

EASY POTATO SKINS

"Put mashed potatoes on the menu and use the skins this way."

Vegetable oil, butter .. **or margarine**	Preheat oven to 475°F. Generously grease jelly roll pans with oil, butter or margarine. Scrub potatoes well. With a paring knife (a vegetable peeler slices too thin), peel skins off the potatoes, about ⅛-inch thick. Place potato pieces in pan, turn to coat both sides, leaving skin-side up. Sprinkle with salt and pepper. Bake for 10 to 12 minutes or until crisp and golden. Serve immediately in a napkin-lined basket.
4 to 6 med. potatoes	
Salt or seasoned salt of your choice	
Freshly ground pepper	

Makes about 4 cups

STORING SNACKS

Snack mixtures containing nuts, seeds and any type of oil or shortening are inclined to turn rancid if exposed to air and heat for a long period of time. This is the reason for storing them in airtight containers in a cool place. Save nut jars, peanut butter jars and other containers with rubber-lined lids for your snacks. Unopened cans or jars of nuts or seeds will keep well on the pantry shelf. Once opened, the refrigerator is the best place to store them. Shelled nuts keep longest in the freezer and will retain their quality for months.

COCONUT CHIPS

"If you have never tackled a whole coconut, do this for fun and enjoy the interesting results."

1 whole fresh .... **coconut**	With a large nail and hammer, puncture the eyes of the coconut. Place upside down in a large strainer and drain into a large measuring cup or medium bowl. (Reserve juice for another use.) Open the shell by hitting firmly with a hammer around widest part of the coconut. Use a small sharp knife to pry out coconut meat and peel off the brown skin. With a vegetable peeler, slice coconut meat into strips.
3 tbsp. butter or ...... **margarine** **Salt**	Preheat oven to 350°F. Melt butter or margarine in a 15½ x 10½ x 1-inch jelly roll pan. Remove from oven and spread coconut slices evenly in the pan. Bake for 10 minutes; toss and bake 6 to 8 minutes longer or until crisped and golden brown. Remove from oven and drain on paper towels. Blot top of coconut with another paper towel to absorb as much grease as possible. Sprinkle lightly with salt. When cool, store loosely covered in a cool place.

Makes about 3 cups

STUFFED DATES

1 pkg. (16 oz.) .... **pitted dates**	Using a small sharp knife dipped in cold water, cut an opening across each date.
1 pkg. (3 oz.) cream .. **cheese, softened** **¼ c. chunky peanut butter**	In a small bowl, mix cream cheese and peanut butter with a fork until blended. Form small balls using about ½ teaspoon of mixture for each. Press a ball into the opening of each date; cover and chill for about 1 hour.

Makes 40 to 42

NOTES: _____

SOFT PRETZELS

1 c. milk	In a small saucepan over medium heat, scald milk with brown sugar, caraway and salt; let cool to lukewarm.
⅓ c. firmly packed dark brown sugar	
2 tsp. caraway seeds	
1 tsp. salt	

1 pkg. active dry yeast	In a small bowl or cup, sprinkle yeast on water; let stand for 5 to 10 minutes or until foamy.
½ c. warm water (105° to 115°F.)	

1½ c. rye flour	In a large mixer bowl at medium speed, beat milk mixture, yeast mixture and rye flour for 1 to 2 minutes or until batter is smooth. Slowly beat in wheat flour for 1 to 2 minutes or until smooth. Stir in ½ cup of the all-purpose flour to make a soft dough that can be handled. On a lightly floured surface, knead in remaining flour until smooth and satiny.
1½ c. whole wheat flour	
1 c. all-purpose flour	

Line baking sheets with foil; grease and dust with flour. Divide dough into four equal portions. Roll one portion into a 12 x 9-inch rectangle. Cut dough into twelve strips, 9 x 1-inch each. Roll each strip into a 15-inch rope and form into a pretzel shape.

Preheat oven to 400° F. Over medium-high heat, bring a medium sauce-pan of water to a boil. With a slotted spoon, lower pretzels, one at a time, into the boiling water for 3 to 4 seconds (longer will make pretzels soggy). Remove and shake off excess water. Place pretzels on baking sheets about 1 inch apart.

1 egg white, lightly ... beaten	Brush with egg white and sprinkle with salt. Bake for 12 to 15 minutes or until golden brown. Cool on wire racks. Repeat with remaining portions of dough. Store in an airtight container in a cool place.
Coarse salt or regular table salt	

Makes 48

PARTY SNACK MIX

½ c. butter or .... In a large skillet over low heat, melt butter or
    margarine   margarine. Stir in Worcestershire sauce, onion
2 tbsp. Worcester-   and celery salts and dry mustard.
    shire sauce
1 tsp. onion salt
½ tsp. celery salt
½ tsp. dry mustard

2 c. bite-size .... Stir in wheat and oat cereals, pretzels and pea-
    shredded wheat   nuts. Stir over low heat for 5 minutes or until
    cereal   mixture is well coated. Cool on paper towels.
2 c. round oat cereal Store in an airtight container in a cool place.
1 c. pretzel sticks
1 c. salted peanuts

Makes about 5 cups

CHEESE CRISPIES

½ c. butter or .... Preheat oven to 350°F. In a small mixer bowl at
    margarine   low speed, beat butter or margarine and cheese
1 c. finely shredded until blended. With motor running, slowly beat in
    sharp Cheddar   flour and red pepper for 1 to 2 minutes or until well
    cheese (4 oz.)   blended.
¾ c. all-purpose flour
⅛ to ¼ tsp. ground
    red pepper

1 c. crisp rice cereal.. Stir in cereal, nuts and chives until well blended.
¼ c. finely chopped   Roll into balls using 1 teaspoon of the mixture per
    nuts   ball and place on ungreased baking sheets.* Bake
2 tsp. chopped chives for 15 to 18 minutes or until bottoms are golden.
                    Cool on wire racks. Store in airtight containers
                    in a cool place.

*Crispies can be frozen on baking sheets, then stored in freezer bags until ready to bake.

Makes about 70

NOTES:

BRIDGE NIBBLES

"This is one of the easiest mixes to put together."

1 c. roasted peanuts..	In a medium bowl, mix nuts, raisins, mixed fruit,
1 c. toasted chopped	seeds or kernels and optional coconut. Store in an
Brazil nuts or	airtight container in a cool place.
whole cashews	
1 c. golden raisins	
1 c. chopped mixed	
dried fruit	
½ c. pumpkin seeds or	
sunflower kernels	
½ c. dried coconut	
chips (optional)	

Makes 5 cups

TOASTING NUTS

Spread nuts, either halved, sliced, slivered, chopped or ground, in a shallow baking pan. Place in a preheated 350°F. oven for 10 to 20 minutes, watching carefully for even browning. Turn the pan or stir the nuts if they are browning too much in one spot. Sesame seeds can be toasted in the same way for about 10 minutes.

CHOW MEIN SNACK

½ c. butter or	In a large skillet over low heat, melt butter. Stir
margarine	in soy sauce, onion powder, lemon pepper and garlic
2 tbsp. soy sauce	powder until well blended.
½ tsp. onion powder	
½ tsp. lemon pepper	
¼ tsp. garlic powder	
2 c. chow mein	Add noodles, corn and oat cereals and optional
noodles	peanuts. Stir over low heat for 2 to 3 minutes or
2 c. bite-size crispy	until moisture is absorbed. Cool on paper towels.
corn cereal	Store in an airtight container in a cool place.
squares	
2 c. round oat cereal	
1 c. unsalted peanuts	
(optional)	

Makes 6 cups

chapter 6 CONTENTS

Beverages *Page*

Pictured on the preceding page is Wassail.

Beverages

WASSAIL

2 qt. apple cider	In a heavy 6-quart saucepan, mix cider, apples,
5 sm. cooking apples, cored	brown sugar, cloves, allspice, cinnamon and nutmeg. Over medium-high heat, bring to a boil; reduce
¼ c. firmly packed brown sugar	heat to low and simmer for 15 minutes.
8 whole cloves	
8 whole allspice	
3 sticks (3″ ea.) cinnamon	
⅛ tsp. ground nutmeg	
1 lemon, thinly	Turn apples. Add lemon and orange slices. Simmer
sliced	15 minutes longer.
1 orange, thinly sliced	
2 c. apple brandy	Just before serving, add optional brandy. To serve,
(optional)	transfer apples and some orange or lemon slices to a
Cinnamon sticks	heated large crock; pour wassail over fruit. Serve in punch cups or mugs with cinnamon stick stirrers.

Makes about 13 (5-ounce) servings

KEEPING HOT PUNCHES HOT

An ordinary punch bowl does not work very well for hot drinks. I have found two excellent serving containers that keep hot drinks hot and are convenient for serving a crowd. One is the slow cooker and the other is the large party percolator. If you are using the slow cooker, it may be best to brew and heat the punch on top of the stove and then transfer it to the slow cooker to keep it hot for serving. Some punches can be brewed in the electric percolator, placing the whole spices and citrus peel or slices in the coffee basket. If this is not appropriate, simply pour the hot punch into the percolator. Do not use the basket or stem; just plug it in to keep the beverage hot.

HOT BUTTERED RUM

"Keep this mixture on hand and stir up hot drinks as needed."

1 c. real butter, at ..... room temperature	In a small mixer bowl at high speed, beat butter until fluffy. Gradually beat in brown sugar, then honey and spices until well blended.
1 c. firmly packed brown sugar	
¼ c. honey	
2 tsp. ground cinnamon	
1 tsp. ground nutmeg	
½ tsp. ground cloves	

Boiling water	To make one serving, place ¼ cup mixture in a warm 10-ounce mug; pour in ½ cup boiling water, stirring to dissolve mixture. Add 3 tablespoons rum and fill with additional boiling water; stir. Make additional servings as described. Add optional whole cloves (three or four per serving) or a sprinkling of nutmeg. Stir with a cinnamon stick. Cover and chill any unused butter mixture up to one month.
3 c. dark rum	
Whole cloves or freshly grated nutmeg (optional)	
Cinnamon sticks	

Makes 8 (10-ounce) servings

GLOGG

1 qt. water	In a heavy 6-quart saucepan, mix water, sugar, raisins, cinnamon, cloves and ginger. Over medium-high heat, bring to a boil; reduce heat to low and simmer for 15 minutes.
1¼ c. sugar	
¾ c. raisins	
5 sticks (3" ea.) cinnamon, broken	
30 whole cloves	
3 tbsp. chopped candied ginger	

3 bottles (750 ml. ..... ea.) red Burgundy	Add Burgundy and orange and lemon slices. Simmer for 15 minutes.
2 oranges, thinly sliced	
1 lemon, thinly sliced	

1¼ c. whole .... blanched almonds	Just before serving, add almonds and raisins. Serve hot in punch cups or mugs.
½ c. raisins	

Makes about 20 (5-ounce) servings

NOTES:

STRAWBERRY MARGARITA

1 pkg. (10 oz.) frozen.. Place strawberries, tequila, lime juice and powdered
   strawberries, sugar in a blender container; cover and blend for
   partially thawed 1 minute or until well blended.
½ **c. tequila**
3 **tbsp. fresh lime juice**
1 **tsp. powdered sugar**

   Crushed ice .... Pour over crushed ice in stemmed glasses. Garnish
4 **lime slices** with lime.

Makes 4 (4-ounce) servings

CARIBBEAN SCREWDRIVER

4 **oz. cream of** .... In a cocktail pitcher or 2-cup measure, mix cream
   coconut* of coconut, orange juice and vodka. Pour into two
4 **oz. orange juice** on-the-rocks glasses filled with ice cubes.
4 **oz. vodka**
   Ice cubes

*Available in liquor stores or the specialty section of your supermarket.

Makes 2 (6-ounce) servings

GARNISHING DRINKS

A pretty garnish will make your drinks taste even better. Choose according to the flavor of the drink. A sweet, fruity drink is enhanced by citrus wedges or slices, fresh berries, mint sprigs, cherries or mixed fruit kabobs. A vegetable or beef-based drink can be perked up with celery or carrot sticks, olives or cocktail onions. Some hot drinks are nicer with a candy cane or cinnamon stick stirrer; pick a compatible flavor. Citrus peel studded with whole cloves adds flavor and color to hot spicy or fruity punches.

PINK CHAMPAGNE WEDDING PUNCH

6 pink rose buds ..... Pour water into a 4½-cup ring mold to a depth
with leaves, of ¾-inch. Evenly distribute roses and leaves in
unsprayed mold. Freeze. Fill mold with water. Freeze again.

1 can (12 oz.) .... In a chilled punch bowl, mix lemonade concentrate,
frozen pink cold water, champagne and soda. Stir gently.
lemonade con-
centrate, thawed Dip ice ring in warm water and unmold. Float
4½ c. cold water flower-side up in punch. Serve in punch cups or
1 bottle (750 ml.) champagne glasses.
pink cham-
pagne, chilled
1 bottle (28 oz.)
lemon-lime
soda, chilled

Makes about 28 (5-ounce) servings

WHITE SANGRIA

¾ c. sugar .... In a large bowl, dissolve sugar in orange liqueur. Add
1½ c. orange liqueur wine and fruit. Cover and chill at least 1 hour.
3 bottles (750 ml. ea.)
dry white wine
4 limes, thinly sliced
3 oranges, thinly sliced
3 lemons, thinly sliced

Ice ring (see below).. To serve, place ice ring in a punch bowl, add wine
1 bottle (28 oz.) mixture and club soda. Stir gently until blended.
club soda, chilled Serve in stemmed glasses.

Makes 18 (6-ounce) servings

MAKING AN ICE RING

Ice rings are popular for punch bowls as decorations and for chilling. Since you want to avoid watering down the punch flavor, use ginger ale or clear fruit juices instead of water. Pour the liquid into a ring mold to a depth of ¾-inch. Freeze solid. Arrange fruits, unsprayed leaves and rose buds or mint sprigs over the frozen liquid. Carefully pour in another ¼-inch of liquid and freeze again to hold decorations in place. When solid, fill the ring mold with liquid and freeze until ready to use. Unmold by dipping mold into a bowl of warm water. Invert frozen ring into well-chilled punch.

TOMATO TORO

1 can (12 oz.) .... In a medium saucepan,
    vegetable juice mix vegetable juice cock-
    cocktail tail, beef broth, lemon
1 can (10½ oz.) juice, sugar, Worcester-
    condensed beef shire sauce and celery
    broth salt. Over medium heat,
1½ tsp. fresh lemon bring to a boil; reduce
    juice heat to low and simmer for
½ tsp. sugar 15 minutes. Serve in mugs
½ tsp. Worcestershire with celery stick stirrers.
    sauce
¼ tsp. celery salt
Celery sticks

Makes 4 (6-ounce) servings

EXTRA-RICH EGGNOG

½ tsp. unflavored ..... In a small saucepan, mix gelatin and ½ cup whipping
    gelatin cream; let stand for 1 minute. Stir over medium heat
1 c. whipping cream until gelatin dissolves. Add remaining cream and
cool to room temperature.

6 eggs .... In a large mixer bowl at high speed, beat eggs and
½ c. sugar sugar until thick and lemon-colored. Add cream
½ c. rum or bourbon mixture, optional rum or bourbon and vanilla. Beat
    (optional) well. Cover and chill until ready to serve.*
1 tsp. vanilla extract

Ground nutmeg .... Serve in punch cups. Sprinkle with nutmeg.

*Can be made up to 3 hours ahead.

Makes 5 (5-ounce) servings

PLANNING YOUR LIQUID REFRESHMENTS

In estimating beverage requirements for a party, it is far better to have too
much than too little. A good rule of thumb is to plan on one drink per
person every 20 to 30 minutes. For a two-hour period, you would need at
least four mixed alcoholic drinks per person, one-half bottle of wine or 2
cups of punch. This will vary according to your guests, the time of day and
the time of year. The standard jigger measure is 1½ ounces. Use the
following as your purchasing guide: 1 pint = 10 jiggers; 1 fifth = 17 jiggers; 1
quart = 21 jiggers. Make or buy plenty of ice cubes. You will need three to
four cubes for each mixed drink.

CREAMY ORANGE SYLLABUB

1 c. whipping . . . . **cream**	Place whipping cream, eggs, breakfast drink powder, tea powder and liqueur in a blender container; cover and blend until smooth. While motor is running, add ice cubes, one at a time, through opening in lid, blending until smooth and frothy.
2 eggs	
¼ c. orange instant breakfast drink powder	
2 tbsp. instant tea powder	
¼ c. orange liqueur	
1 c. ice cubes	
Maraschino . . . . **cherries (optional)** **Orange slices, halved (optional)**	Serve immediately in punch cups or whiskey sour glasses garnished with maraschino cherries and orange slices if desired.

Makes 4 (5-ounce) servings

THE RECIPE

1 pkg. (16 oz.) frozen whole straw- berries, thawed	Drain fruits and reserve syrup. Evenly distribute fruits over the bottom of a 4½-cup ring mold. Freeze. Fill mold with water. Freeze again.
1 pkg. (10 oz.) frozen mixed fruit, thawed	
4 c. water . . . . **2 c. port wine**	In a punch bowl, mix water, wine, lemonade, fruit punch and pineapple juice concentrates, brandy and reserved fruit syrup.
2 cans (12 oz. ea.) frozen lemonade concentrate, par- tially thawed	
1 can (6 oz.) frozen fruit punch con- centrate, partially thawed	
1 can (6 oz.) frozen pineapple juice concentrate, partially thawed	
½ c. brandy	
5 c. ginger ale, ... **chilled**	To serve, add ginger ale. Stir gently. Dip ice ring in warm water and unmold. Float fruit-side up in punch bowl. Serve in punch cups.

Makes about 25 (5-ounce) servings

Index *Recipe photographed